To Educate the Human Potential

Maria Montessori

AAKAR

To Educate the Human Potential
Maria Montessori

© Aakar Books

First Published 1948
First Aakar Edition 2019
Reprinted 2020

ISBN   978-93-5002-617-5

All rights reserved. No part of this book may be reproduced or transmitted, in any form or by any means, without the prior permission of the Publisher.

Published by
AAKAR BOOKS
28 E Pocket IV, Mayur Vihar Phase I
Delhi 110 091 India
aakarbooks@gmail.com

Laser Typeset at
Arpit Printographers, Delhi

Printed at
Sapra Brothers, Noida

Contents

Introduction   7

1. The Six-Year-Old Confronted With the Cosmic Plan   11
2. The Right Use of Imagination   17
3. The New Psychology of the Unconscious   23
4. The Universe Presented to the Child's Imagination   32
5. The Drama of the Ocean   37
6. How Mother Earth has been Created   44
7. A Primeval World War   50
8. The Cretaceous Period   54
9. The Earth in Travail Again   59
10. Early Man   62
11. Nomad versus Settler   67
12. Man: The Creator and Revealer   71
13. Early Great Civilisations   76
14. Egypt Through the Ages   80
15. Life in Babylon, and Her Dealings with Tyre   84
16. Dignity and Impudence   89

17.	The Hellenic Spirit: Creator of Europe	94
18.	Man: Whither Bound	99
19.	Conclusion	106

Introduction

This book is intended to follow *Education for a New World* and to help teachers to envisage the child's needs after the age of six. We claim that the average boy or girl of twelve who has been educated till then at one of our schools knows at least as much as the finished High School product of several years' seniority, and the achievement has been at no cost of pain or distortion to body or mind. Rather are our pupils equipped in their whole being for the adventure of life, accustomed to the free excercise of will and judgement, illuminated by imagination and enthusiasm. Only such pupils can exercise rightly the duties of citizens in a civilised commonwealth.

The first four chapters are mainly psychological, showing the changed personality with which the teacher has to deal at six years of age, and the need for a corresponding change of approach. The secret of success is found to lie in the right use of imagination in awakening interest, and the stimulation of seeds of interest already sown by attractive literary and pictorial material, but all correlated to a central idea, of greatly ennobling inspiration—the Cosmic Plan, in which all, consciously or unconsciously, serve the great Purpose of Life. It is shown how the conception of evolution has been modified of late through geological and biological discoveries, so that self-perfection now has to yield precedence to service among the primary natural urges.

The next eight chapters show how the Cosmic Plan can be presented to the child, as a thrilling tale of the earth we live in, its many changes through slow ages when water was nature's chief toiler for accomplishment of her purposes, how land and sea fought for supremacy, and how equilibrium of elements was achieved, that life might appear on the stage to play its part in the great drama. Illustrated as it must be by fascinating charts and diagrams, the creation of earth as we now know it unfolds before the child's imagination, and always with emphasis on the function each agent has to perform in nature's household, whether consciously or unconsiously, failure in this alone leading to extinction. So the tale proceeds till Paleolithic Man appears, most significantly traced by the tools he used on his environment rather than by physical remains of so slight a creature. The new element of mind is brought to creation by man, and from that time the children are helped to see the great acceleration that has taken place in evolution. They learn to revere the earliest pioneers, who toiled for purposes unknown to them but now to be recognised. Nomadic men and settlers alike contributed to build up early communities, and by interchanges of war and peace to share and spread social amenities.

From Chapter 13 brief descriptions are given of some of the earliest civilisations, particularly with a view to their impacts on each other, showing human society as slowly organising itself towards unity, just as, in the individual human being, organs are built around separate centres of interest, to be later connected by the blood-circulatory system and the nerves, into an integrated human organism. So the child is led, by review of some of the most thrilling epochs of world history, to see that so far humanity has been in an embryonic stage, and that it is just now emerging into true birth, able to consciously realise its true unity and function.

The last chapters go back to the psychological point of view, urging on educators the supreme importance, to the nation and to the world, of the tasks imposed on them. Not in the service of any political or social creed should the teacher work, but in the service of the complete human being, able to exercise in freedom a self-disciplined will and judgment, unperverted by prejudice and undistorted by fear.

1
The Six-Year-Old Confronted With the Cosmic Plan

Education between the ages of six and twelve is not a direct continuation of what has gone before, though to be built upon that basis. Psychologically there is a decided change in personality, and we recognise that natue has made this a period for the acquisition of culture, just as the former was for the absorption of environment. We are confronted with a considerable development of consciousness that has already taken place, but now that consciousness is thrown outwards with a special direction, intelligence being extroverted, and there is an unusual demand on the part of the child to know the reasons of things. Knowledge can be best given where there is eagerness to learn, so this is the period when the seed of everything can be sown, the child's mind being like a fertile field, ready to receive what will germinate into culture. But if neglected during this period, or frustrated in its vital needs, the child's mind becomes artificially dulled, henceforth to resist imparted knowledge. Interest will no longer be there if the seed is sown too late, but at six years of age all items of culture are received enthusiastically, and later these seeds will expand and grow. If asked how many seeds may be sown, my answer is: "As many as possible." Looking around us at the cultural development of our epoch of evolution, we see no limit to what must be offered to the child, for his will be an immense field of chosen activity, and he should not be hampered by ignorance. But to give the whole of modern culture has become an impossibility, and so a need arises for a special method, whereby all factors of culture may be introduced to the six-year-old; not in a syllabus to be imposed on him, or with exactitude of detail, but in the broadcasting of the maximum number of seeds of interest. These will be held lightly in the mind, but will be capable of later germination, as the will becomes more directive, and thus he may become an individual suited to these expansive times.

A second side of education at this age concerns the child's exploration of the moral field, discrimination between good and evil. He is no longer receptive, absorbing impressions with ease, but wants to understand for himself, not content with accepting mere facts. As moral activity develops, he wants to use his own judgment, which will often be quite different from that of his teachers. There is nothing more difficult than to teach moral values to a child of this age; he gives an immediate retort to everything that we say, having become a rebel. Mothers often feel hurt because their children, formerly all love and affection, have become impertinent and rudely domineering. An inner change has taken place, but nature is quite logical in arousing now in the child not only a hunger for knowledge and understanding, but a claim to mental independence, a desire to distinguish good from evil by his own powers, and to resent limitation by arbitrary authority. In the field of morality, the child now stands in need of his own inner light.

Yet a third interesting fact to be observed in the child of six is his need to associate himself with others, not merely for the sake of company, but in some sort of organised activity. He wants to mix with others in a group wherein each has a different status. A leader is chosen, and is obeyed, and a strong group is formed. This is a natural tendency, through which mankind becomes organised. If during this period of social interest and mental acuteness all possibilities of culture are offered to the child, to widen his outlook and ideas of the world, this organisation will be formed and will develop; the amount of light a child has acquired in the moral field, and the lofty ideals he has formed, will be made useful for purposes of social organisation at a later stage.

All other factors however sink into insignificance beside the importance of feeding the hungry intelligence, and opening vast fields of knowledge to eager exploration. If we set about this task without any method, we will find it absolutely impossible to accomplish. But we are already in possession of the secret by which the problem can be solved, having been initiated into it by the child himself in his earlier years. We are not unknown to him nor he to us, and we have learnt from his certain fundamental principles of psychology. One is that the child must learn by his own individual activity, being given a mental freedom to take what he needs, and not to be questioned in his choice. Our teaching must only answer the mental needs of the child, never dictate them. Just as a small child cannot be still because he is in need of coordinating his movements, so the older child, who seems troublesome being curious over the what, why and wherefore of everything he sees, is building up his mind by this mental activity, and must be given a wide field of culture on which to feed. The task of teaching becomes easy, since we do not need to choose what we shall teach, but should place all before him for the satisfaction of his mental appetite. He must have absolute freedom of choice, and then he requires nothing but repeated experiences which will become increasingly marked by interest and serious attention, during his acquisition of some desired knowledge.

The child of six who has been in a Montessori school has the advantage of not being so ignorant as the child who has missed that experience. He knows how to read and write, has an interest in mathematics, science, geography and history, so that it is easy to introduce him to any amount of further knowledge. The teacher is confronted with an individual who has already acquired the basis of culture, and is anxious to build on it, to learn and penetrate deeper into any matter of interest. How clearly then lies the path before the teacher; it would almost seem that he has nothing to do. Not so; the teacher's task is no small or easy one. He has to prepare a vast amount of knowledge to satisfy the child's mental hunger, and he is not, like the ordinary teacher, limited by a syllabus, prescribing just so much of every subject to be imparted within a set time, and on no account to be exceeded. The child's needs are clearly more difficult to answer, and the teacher can no longer defend himself behind syllabus and timetable. He has himself to acquire a reasonable acquaintance with every subject, and even then only the outer shell of the problem will have been pierced. But let him take courage, for he will not be without help, and a scientifically devised and tested plan.

Since it is considered to be necessary to give so much to the child, let us give him a vision of the whole universe. The universe is an imposing reality, and an answer to all questions. We shall walk together on this path of life, for all things are part of the universe, and are connected with each other to form one whole unity. This idea helps the mind of the child to become fixed, to stop wandering in an aimless quest for knowledge. He is satisfied, having found the universal centre of himself with all things.

It is certainly necessary to centralise the interest of the child, but the usual methods today are not effective to that end. How can the mind of a growing individual continue to be interested if all our teaching is around one particular subject of limited scope, and is confined to the transmission of such small details of knowledge as he is able to memorise? How can we force the child to be interested when interest can only arise from within? It is only duty and fatigue which can be induced from without, never interest. That point must be very clear.

If the idea of the universe is presented to the child in the right way, it will do more for him than just arouse his interest, for it will create in him admiration and wonder, a feeling loftier than any interest and more satisfying. The child's mind then will no longer wander, but becomes fixed and can work. The knowledge he then acquires is organised and systematic; his intelligence becomes whole and complete because of the vision of the whole that has been presented to him, and his interest spreads to all, for all are linked and have their place in the universe on which his mind is centred. The stars, earth, stones, life of all kinds form a whole in relation with each other, and so close is this relation that we cannot understand a stone without some understanding of the great sun. No matter what we touch, an atom, or a cell, we cannot explain it without knowledge of the wide universe. What better answer can we give to those questers for knowledge? It becomes doubtful whether even the universe will suffice. How did it come into being, and how will it end? A greater curiosity arises, which can never be satiated; so will last through a lifetime. The laws governing the universe can be made interesting and wonderful to the child, more interesting even than things in themselves, and he begins to ask: What am I? What is the task of man in this wonderful universe? Do we merely live here for ourselves, or is there something more for us to do? Why do we struggle and fight? What is good and evil? Where will it all end?"

This plan of cosmic education as a foundation stone of the advanced method was first explained in England in 1935, and it has already proved itself to be the only path on which our feet can firmly tread in further educational research. It cannot be used with the wholly illiterate or ignorant, but it is received with joy by the child who has indirectly been prepared for it in the Montessori school. Truly it is no new idea, for it has been the natural plan wherever there has been education in the real sense of the word, though lately fallen into disuse, for children first to be taught the creation of the world, and man's place in it, so far as these questions could be answered in the light of religion and philosophy. The answer was always what it still is, "God has sent you on the earth to work and do your duty." This principle can now, however, be developed on a scientific plan, and be made far more attractive.

2

The Right Use of Imagination

The six-year-old who comes from a Montessori class, for whom primarily this further course is devised, already possesses many cultural interests, and has a sort of deep passion for order and even for mathematics, so often regarded as an obstacle to the average child. Moreover his hand is already controlled, possessed and directed by the mind in minute movements. The practical work done in our early schools found such public approbation that our scientific manual exercises have largely been adopted by schools professing other methods regarding most aspects of education. In this more advanced period we continue to give children the opportunity to learn through the activity of the hand, especially in mechanics and physics. For instance, the children learn the laws of pressure and tension by being asked to build an arch of stones, so placed as to hold together without need of cement. By building bridges, aeroplanes, railroads (calculating the curvature), they become familiar with the principles of Statics and Dynamics as part of the daily school routine, wherever our method is properly applied with full equipment. Wherever possible mechanical contrivances are introduced for every detail of practical life, that our children may be fitted to take part in a civilisation which is entirely based on machines.

In their adoption of this part of our method some modern schools, especially in the United States, have gone too far, so that children in this intellectual stage of growth are made to occupy themselves solely with these machines, devised as they are for developing intelligence. In such schools freedom too has entered with the machines, children being allowed to choose their work, which is so far good. But whatever cannot be learnt in this way is barred out, as insignificant and negligible, as mathematics and other abstract subjects, considered as beyond the child's comprehension by free and spontaneous activity. Those schools based on practical work are opposed to the so-called "old-fashioned" schools where mainly abstract subjects are taught and facts memorised; but we oppose both alike.

Personality is one and indivisible, and all mental attitudes depend on one centre. This is the secret which the small child has himself revealed to us by doing work far beyond our dreams and expectations in all fields, including the intellectual and abstract, provided his hand was allowed to work in tandem with the intelligence. Children show a great attachment to the abstract subjects when they arrive at them through manual activity. They proceed to fields of knowledge hitherto held inaccessible to them, as grammar and mathematics. I wonder how the theory arose that in order to work with the hand one must have an uncultivated mind, or that a cultivated mind consorted with manual helplessness. Must a man be classified either as a worker with his head or with his hands, instead of being allowed to function with his whole personality? Where is the logic in the view that one-sided development can be beneficial to the whole? In modern conferences highly distinguished people, who have given their lives to the cause of education, seriously discuss which is to be preferred, the practical method or an intellectual discipline. But to us the children have themselves revealed that discipline is the result of an entire development only, of mental functioning aided by manual activity. Allow the whole to function together and there is discipline, but otherwise not. Tribes, groups and nations are the results of such spontaneous discipline and association. There is only one problem, and it is human development in its totality; once this is achieved in any unit—child or nation—everything else follows spontaneously and harmoniously.

Being persuaded then that the whole personality must be engaged, and that it needs centralising first by the cosmic idea, the question arises as to how and when the idea should be presented. From the smaller children we have learnt the effectiveness of an indirect approach, as by addressing older children in their presence, for in our schools the ages are, to a limited extent, mixed. When we try to show something to the older children, the younger ones crowd around showing eager interest. The interest has been especially shown by a child of six towards a chart illustrating the relative sizes of the sun and the earth by globe and point. The younger children were thrilled by the realisation that this invoked in them, and were unable to tear themselves away, though the older child for whom the instruction was planned found it rather commonplace, and needed some other things to arouse in him a similar interest. There is a difference between such enthusiasm and mere understanding. The point and the sphere touched the imagination of the younger child, leaving him full of enthusiasm for something beyond his former limits, belonging not to the physical environment, which is not possible to be grasped by hand. If moreover this particular illustration left the older child unmoved, it was not that nothing had the power similarly to touch his imagination, bearing him beyond his limited world into wider realms, by great strides into the unknown universe; but he could not reach without help such marvels and mysteries. It is along this path of the higher realities, which can be grasped by imagination, that the child is led between the ages of six and twelve. Imaginative vision is quite different from mere perception of an object, for it has no limits. Not only can imagination travel through infinite space, but also through infinite time; we can go backwards through the epochs, and have the vision of the earth as it was, with the creatures that inhabited it. To make it clear whether or not a child has understood, we should see whether he can form a vision of it within the mind, whether he has gone beyond the level of mere understanding.

Human consciousness comes into the world as a flaming ball of imagination. Everything invented by man, physical or mental, is the fruit of someone's imagination. In the study of history and geography we are helpless without imagination, and when we propose to introduce the universe to the child, what but imagination can be of use to us? I consider it a crime to present such subjects as may be noble and creative aids to the imaginative faculty in such a manner as to deny its use, and on the other hand to require the child to memorise what he has not been able to visualise. These subjects must be presented so as to touch the imagination of the child, and make him enthusiastic, and then add fuel to the burning fuel that has been lit.

The secret of good teaching is to regard the child's intelligence as a fertile field in which seeds may be sown, to grow under the heat of flaming imagination. Our aim therefore is not merely to make the child understand, and still less to force him to memorise, but so to touch his imagination as to enthuse him to his inmost core. We do not want complacent pupils, but eager ones; we seek to sow life in the child rather than theories, to help him in his growth, mental and emotional as well as physical, and for that we must offer grand and lofty ideas to the human mind, which we find ever ready to receive them, demanding more and more.

Educationists in general agree that imagination is important, but they would have it cultivated as separate from intelligence, just as they would separate the latter from the activity of the hand. They are the vivisectionists of the human personality. In the school they want children to learn dry facts of reality, while their imagination is cultivated by fairy-tales, concerned with a world that is certainly full of marvels, but not the world around them in which they live. Certainly these tales have impressive factors which move the childish mind to pity and horror, for they are full of woe and tragedy, of children who are starved, ill-treated, abandoned and betrayed. Just as adults find pleasure in tragic drama and literature, these tales of goblins and monsters give pleasure and stir the child's imagination, but they have no connection with reality.

On the other hand, by offering the child the story of the universe, we give him something a thousand times more infinite and mysterious to reconstruct with his imagination, a drama no fable can reveal. If imagination is educated merely by fairy-tales, at most the pleasure it gives will be continued later in novel-reading, but we should never so limit its education. A mind that is used to seek pleasure only in fantastic tales slowly but surely becomes lazy, incapable of nobler preoccupations. In social life we find too many examples of this sloth of mind, people caring only to be well-dressed, gossip with friends and go to the cinema. Their intelligence is hopelessly buried under barriers which cannot now be removed. Their interest becomes increasingly narrow, till it is centred round the petty self, excluding the wonders of the world and sympathy with suffering humanity. Theirs is a veritable death in life.

3

The New Psychology of the Unconscious

Since the beginning of the twentieth century, a great change has taken place in psychological study, and very significantly the new psychologists are in conflict with the established methods of education, though unable themselves to conceive how schools are to be induced to follow the new lines. But actually this new trend has already found expression in our schools, with which the older psychological theories have nothing to do, either in practice or organisation. Modern psychology exactly suits our method, for whereas the older science was based on the observation of superficial facts of consciousness, the new seeks to observe the unconscious mind, and probe its secret in order to discover the mind's relation to the facts of life.

Older psychologists made a strong distinction between the facts of life and psychological factors, keeping them poles apart; but explorers of the field of the unconscious have discovered that the study of the latter can be placed on the same footing as biological factors, and that moreover the mind is a unity, a whole, not divisible into a number of separate mental faculties, such as Memory, Reason, Attention and Association of Ideas, each to be consciously trained. Education used to concern itself mainly with the separate training of attention, or the power of reasoning in order to grasp what is taught, and Will, the voluntary effort to learn, and the mind was viewed as superior to the vital instincts, to be impressed and trained from without. Today the mind is thought of as one whole, not as separate mental faculties, and vitally connected with the whole personality; thus modern psychology forms as complement to our method of education.

In accordance with these new ways of thought, we are concerned with three main mental factors, of which the first is the vital elements, part of life itself. This has the power of retaining part of all experiences that the individual has undergone, and it is not peculiar to human beings, but is the same with all living creatures. In order to gain something from life, we must retain traces of experiences undergone, and here comes memory to our aid. But we soon realise the shortcomings of conscious memory, how blurred and indefinite are its impressions. Modern psychology however affirms that the unconscious or subconscious mind remembers everything, so memory now takes on the aspect of a vast mystery, needing close study for its elucidation.

This subconscious memory has marvellous mobility, and everything is there on record though we are not consciously aware of it. Thus there is a racial memory, by the help of which all living beings reproduce their own species, and perpetuate manners of living. By it birds are enabled to build their nests according to the traditional manner of their kind. This greater memory is called the 'Mneme,' and it is that by which a child unconsciously recognises the sounds of human speech, and retains those sounds for imitation. Only a very small part of the mneme penetrates the conscious limits, and that part is what we call memory. All the experiences through which an individual passes in life are retained in the mneme, not only the infinitesimal part that enters the consciousness.

For an easy experiment in psychology, a person may be asked to memorise a list of detached syllables, and to repeat the same from memory after a few days' interval since dropping the exercise. He will have forgotten the syllables; but will now be able to memorise them again in a much shorter time, because they were retained in the mneme. It is not an accumulation of memories that is left in the mneme, but a power to recall experiences to the conscious memory from which it has dropped. An educated man may have no memory of many things that he was taught at school, but he has intelligence, a power of quick apprehension on those subjects, which has been retained by the mneme. Thus it is not the experiences in themselves, but the traces of them left behind in the mneme, which make a mind powerful, such traces being known as engrams.

The subconsicous is full of these engrams, by which the intellect grows much more than by conscious memory. By our use of this fact it follows that in our schools the child's intellectual powers become far augmented, whereas in ordinary schools the only object is to store knowledge in the conscious memory, and no opportunity is given to the child, by continuous and varied experiences, to increase his engrams.

Another vital factor of the mind is the urge to carry an action to completion, and it is part of what has been called the 'Elan Vitale.' The philosopher Bergson gave this name to the vital urge which drives every living creature into experiences, for the storing of engrams. This power brings children in our school to work spontaneously, persisting in repeating the same experience, till completely satisfied. It is sometimes called the 'Will to Live,' and in connection with the human being is classed among conscious, psychic factors, while in other living creatures it ranks as biological and subconscious. Truly the Elan Vitale is in every facet of life, and when it emerges into the conscious part of the mind becomes a voluntary factor, as the will. The far greater subconscious vital urge is now called by psychologists the horme, which has a field relatively as vast in extent as compared with that of the conscious will as has the mneme compared with that of memory. Human beings may be forced into action through the horme without the will entering consciously into the action, as in hypnotism, and this is rightly felt to be dangerous to humanity, for these are forces of which we are yet unaware, so accordingly cannot well defend ourselves against them. The inter-relations of minds occupy a most important chapter of human psychology, men often performing acts the reason for which they are quite unable to explain. Certain actions which children perform, with serious reactions on themselves, are of this type, and that the younger generation may grow up better defended against these dangers it is necessary that they be understood, and that the conscious will be from the first rightly developed and exercised, as by the Montessori method of education.

The third important factor in this labyrinth of the subconscious mind is what used to be called the association of ideas, or the principle of sequential formation of thoughts. On this mainly all methods of education have been based; around some initial idea more ideas may be assembled, in tune with or diametrically opposed to that idea. Modern psychologists now regard this as of only secondary importance, and only superficially true. They attach importance less to the ideas than to the engrams, which associate within the subconscious whenever the mind becomes interested in something. This association of engrams is spontaneous, and far more actively powerful and lasting than any induced chain of related ideas. It is well-known that a mathematical student may ponder for hours over some problem without success, till he decides to "sleep on it," and on waking finds a solution easy. Is it because he has rested, and so can understand and think better? No, for immediately on waking he is conscious of the problem being already solved in his mind, as if the solution itself had forced him to wake and register it. It could only happen because the engrams did not sleep, but in association had done the work and forced it into the consciousness.

Thus it may be said that every human being does his most intelligent work in the subconscious, where psychic complexes are the construction of engrams. These do much more than create an association of ideas, for they organise themselves to carry out work which we are unable to consciously. Psychic complexes help a writer to create beautiful ideas, new to his conscious mind and vaguely attributed to inspiration. The working of these complexes is of immense importance in education.

In accordance with these discoveries, we are now advised not to labour at memorising some important piece of work, but rather to con it lightly and then set it aside for some days without quite forgetting it, so allowing the engrams time to organise themselves in concentration. This is exactly what is observed to happen in a Montessori school, where children's revelations of their own mental processes have anticipated psychological research. Children are often seen walking alone by themselves while others are working, for just after learning something they feel the need of quiet; on return to the class they will show new ability, just as a child returning to school after holidays finds himself able to understand what was obscure before. In the light of these facts, how futile and even mischievous appears cramming for examinations!

Though we gladly acknowledge these many points of agreement with modern psychologists, whose work is complementary to our own, we yet must disagree with them on one major point. They have hitherto failed in the application of their theories to educational problems, and have become convinced that the application will be achieved only by future generations of men, whereas we know them to be immediately applicable under the right conditions. Psychological study has been pursued outside the schools, conclusions being derived from adult humanity an experimental probing into the unconscious, and they have been disappointed in their expectation that children would react in a special manner when their new methods were practised on them. But we have learnt that child-psychology is not that of the adult, and its essential condition is freedom to act in a prepared environment where the child can be intelligently active. As long as teachers thrust their conclusions on the child, however sound their study of psychology in the abstract may be, they will never attain their end, which is the child's spontaneous interest and application. Thus, much has been said of late, following psychoanalysis, of the sublimation of the instincts, and they have sought to accomplish this by the cultivation of sentiment and the emotions, but school children prove unresponsive. Psychologists base their theories on animal behaviour and on adult response to psycho-analysis, and move forward towards educational reform, joining us at a certain point on the way, as we proceed starting from the child himself. They seek a method of education to suit their theory, while we seek a psychological theory to suit our method.

As an example of this sublimation of the instincts, a modern writer has truly said that modern science is a monument to sublimated curiosity. We entirely agree, and have proved that the child may acquire a great interest in science and all its marvels, when given a near vision of the beginning of life, and its progress up to the present day. We see that the child's instinct of curiosity is sublimated by those lofty interests, but only if we present them to him at a far earlier age than the psychologist would deem possible. The child has taught us that in this early stage only is he specially endowed with an acuter sensibility and interest than he will show later, when he will be able to study scientifically and precisely only if already equipped with an emotion and sentiment for those subjects. He will then no longer possess mere curiosity, but an intense interest, an enthusiasm based on emotion.

The child should love everything that he learns, for his mental and emotional growths are linked. Whatever is presented to him must be made beautiful and clear, striking his imagination. Once this love has been kindled, all problems confronting the educationist will disappear. The great Italian poet, Dante, has said: "La somma sapienza e il primo amore," or "The greatest wisdom is first to love." To sublimate the soul one has to reach this perfect state of love—what has been called Intellectual Love, to distinguish it from the personal. Children can and do love abstract subjects, such as mathematics, so love can exist for the mental work, and the psychologist's dream for the future has already been achieved.

It is hoped that when this sentiment of love for all subjects can be aroused in children, people in general will become more human, and brutal wars will come to an end. But a love for science and art, and all that mankind has created, will not suffice to make men and women love one another. To love a beautiful sunset, or to look with wonder on a tiny insect, does not necessarily awaken a greater feeling of affection towards humanity, nor does a love for art in a man beget a love for his neighbour. What is very necessary is that the individual from the earliest years should be placed in relation with humanity. There is no love in our hearts for the human beings from whom we have received, and are receiving so much, in bread and clothing, and numerous inventions for our benefit. We take and enjoy all that is done for us without gratitude, like atheists who withhold their gratitude and love from God. Perhaps we teach the child to thank God and pray to Him, but not to thank humanity, God's prime agent in creation; we give no thought to the men and women who daily give their lives that we may live more richly. The child will have the greater pleasure in all subjects, and find them easier to learn, if he is led to realise how these subjects first came to be studied and who studied them. We write and read, and the child can be taught who invented writing and the instruments wherewith we write, how printing came and books became so numerous. Every achievement has come by the sacrifice of someone now dead. Every map speaks eloquently of the work of explorers and pioneers, who underwent hardships and trials to find new places, rivers and lakes, and to make the world greater and richer for our dwelling.

Let us in education ever call the attention of children to the hosts of men and women who are hidden from the light of fame, so kindling a love of humanity; not the vague and anaemic sentiment preached today as brotherhood, nor the political sentiment that the working classes should be redeemed and uplifted. What is first wanted is no patronising charity for humanity, but a reverent consciousness of its dignity and worth. This should be cultivated in the same way as a religious sentiment, which indeed should be in us all, for we should not need to be reminded that no man can love God while remaining indifferent to his neighbour.

4

The Universe Presented to the Child's Imagination

To interest the children in the universe, we must not begin by giving them elementary facts about it, to make them merely understand its mechanism, but start with far loftier notions of a philosophical nature, put in an acceptable manner, suited to the child's psychology. Here we may usefully call to aid some myths or fairytales, but they must be such as symbolise truths of nature, not the wholly fantastic.

We can talk of earth in its three coverings of solid, liquid and gaseous, and a fourth covering, that is the envelop of life, occupying the whole outer atmosphere as well as penetrating the three coverings themselves. It is sometimes called the 'biosphere', or sphere of life, and it is as intimately part of the earth as the fur is of an animal, not something which suddenly rained on the world from outside. Part, then, of the earth's body, like an animal's fur is essentially one with it, its function is to grow with it, not only for itself, but for earth's upkeep and transformation. Life is one of the creative forces of the world; it is an energy, with its special laws that are studied in biology, just as there are laws governing physical and chemical changes. We have already learnt that life has a tendency to activity, and that it has the power to acquire and retain impressions. These are the powers which build something new for the mind, as studied in psychology, and as fundamental energies they are the chief powers of life. The impulse to activity leads to experience, which is retained by the mental organism. In animals and in men alike mneme and horme work in their different fields, mental and physical, and while in its functions life tends to its own upkeep, it is at the same time being led by its experiences to a perfection of being, the process of self-perfecting being called evolution.

Just as the animal's fur grows and changes with the growth of the animal, just as the feathers of a fledgeling gain beauty of form and colour as the bird gains maturity, so also life undergoes changes together with the evolution of the earth. It is not that life needs to attain a perfection for itself, but being an intrinsic part of creation, it does its part in transforming the world, its variations being more related to the earth's needs than to its own urge to perfection.

Life is a cosmic agent. How will this truth be presented to the children so as to strike their imagination? Perhaps the child is likely to be most impressed by size, and the tremendous extent and magnitude of life on the globe may easily be introduced, because he already has in his possession the power of numbers. First he may be given the figures of the human population in every country, these being easily obtained, and then let us pass on to life in the depths of ocean, which are known to be incalculable. First we deal with those impressive giants of the sea, the whales, which must logically, from their size, be much fewer in number than the smaller fish. Whales live in herds in the northern seas, but swim in the cold season to the warmer regions, where they are joined by other groups, as the sperm whales, from the Antarctic. Their herds can then be counted not by hundreds, but by thousands of hundreds, so we can imagine the rest of the life of the sea, consisting of myriads of swarms of lesser creatures. We need the help of numbers for painting the imaginative picture, and if statistics are not available we can speak in terms of the areas covered in some seas where fishes at certain seasons are thrown up to the surface. They have been known at such times to cover an area of thirty to forty square miles, and those are only the few that come to the surface from a submarine disturbance. Further, when we find that from a comparatively small region it takes as many as 10,000 boats to bring to land the yearly haul of fish, and that the sale in Europe alone of just one sort of fish, the cod, amounts to 40 million a year, we begin to realise something of the extent of marine life. Again, consider the rates of breeding, the herring laying 70,000 eggs at a time, and the cod laying a million twice a year, and prolonging its life normally ten years to do it.

Children like to work out these colossal figures, and may then be told that fish belong to the aristocracy of life, and that the lower orders are yet far more prolific, not even the extremest limits of numbers sufficing to count them. Jelly fish are known sometimes to swarm to the surface in such numbers that the fastest of steamers takes three days to go through them, and these vast hordes themselves live by feeding on the far more numerous smaller living creatures, which they catch with their innumerable tentacles, but which in number seem inexhaustible. We can imagine how many there must be of those microscopic creatures that light up miles and miles of a tropic sea with phosphoresence, rivalling the stars on a clear night. In a single drop of water under the microscope one can detect hundreds of minute living things, so what must be their number in the great ocean? It has been estimated that one of the smallest of these marine lives can produce a million individuals like himself in 10 days. So after 20 days there may be a million million from this one tiny creature, and the cube, of a million in a month.

Similar discoveries have been made in the plant and animal life on land. Livingstone, the great explorer, counted 40,000 antelopes in a herd that passed him in Central Africa. In the air, a flock of pigeons in flight has been known to obscure the light of the sun, and certain marine birds in South America are so numerous that their excreta, left behind on cliffs where they rest, forms a valuable article of commerce called 'Guano'. Swarms of locusts are a pest in many lands, clearing every ear of grain as they pass over fields in their flight, and leaving famine in their wake. In plant life numbers are still less calculable; there are forests where the undergrowth is so thickly impenetrable that even the animals have to make their way over tree-tops in search of food.

Life is adventurous and beset with many dangers, in sea and air as on land. Marine species are under constant threat of extermination by the voracious appetites of larger creatures, themselves victimised in turn. On land, beside these dangers there are famines, floods, eruptions, plagues to take their toll of life, but none of these could be compared with the destruction that would ensure if either air or water were to fail. All life would then be annihilated, in one great masterstroke. Against all other dangers animals are armed by the instinct of self-preservation, so that enough survive to carry on the species, but against deprivation of these indispensable elements no creature has any defence. Further, some people have been alarmed about the danger to the earth from the cooling of the sun, or a possible collision with a comet; but these risks are remote and secondary compared with the failure of air and water.

It seems then that since the remotest beginnings of life on the earth, through great changes when continents have been submerged and the equilibrium of the world shifted, these two elements have remained constant and unchanging in their purity and essential nature, though not necessarily in the forms they now take. It is their purity which must be guarded, and in what does this purity consist? Water is a composite of many elements, and has a minute quantity of a certain salt in the proportion of 7 parts in 100,000. A small quantity like this is innocuous, but if increased to the extent of 40 parts in 100,000, no life could survive. How is it that the sea never gets overcharged with this poison, carbonate of calcium, though rivers are constantly pouring loads into the ocean?

In a similar manner air is found to contain a minute part of a poisonous gas called carbon dioxide, which also would have deadly results if not continuously being modified by the work of other agents. How can we rely on a sure sufficiency of air fit for our breathing, when we know that plants and animals all give off this poisonous gas in breathing, and every decaying body corrupts the atmosphere with it? This atmosphere is only a few miles deep, and is lighter than the deadly gas, which must occupy therefore the lowest part of it, dooming us, it would seem, the more inevitably. But we are not haunted by this danger, are in fact quite unconcerned about it, being assured that God protects us. But the fact is that He works through agents in this protection that He gives to all His children, and we owe them gratitude and some understanding of the part they play, so that we too may learn to do more effectively our share of work in the cosmic plan. Our proud civilisation and all the marvellous achievements of evolution have been made possible by the self-sacrifice of humble saviours of whose work we are unconscious, most of all by those who still continuously purify the air we breathe and the water that is needed for so many vital purposes.

5

The Drama of the Ocean

Creation was no instantaneous act of God, but has unfolded itself continuously in time, and still is unfulfilled, the Sabbath of rest not reached. Since land and water separated and land was channelled by streams for its drainage, rivers have been bearing to ocean quantities of calcareous matter, sufficient to have choked up the ocean in some 6,000 years if left unhindered to that end, and earth and water might have then blended again in a muddy chaos; but that has not happened in 4,000,000 years, for the catastrophe was averted by the activity of living things, who stepped in to the rescue when the laws governing inanimate nature began to prove insufficient.

At the epoch when such a relapse threatened, the kingdom of the sea was ruled by Trilobites of various kinds. These were three-lobed creatures, with many legs and numerous other appendices for swimming purposes. They had evolved quite complex forms, and could be a foot in length. Other proud ocean-dwellers were Cephalopods—literally meaning with legs on their heads—of which the Nautilus is most famous, having inspired the American poet, Oliver Wendel Holmes, by its habit of continually adding larger chambers of its cell, to live in the outermost and most spacious—a symbol of evolution. Taught by the Chambered

Nautilus, the poet adjures himself:
> Build thee more stately mansions, O my soul,
> > As the swift seasons roll!
> > Leave thy low-vaulted past.
> Let each new temple, nobler than the last,
> Shut thee from heaven with a dome more vast,
> > Till thou at last art free,
> Leaving thine outgrown shell by life's unresting sea.

The nautilus had a brain and nervous system, was quite highly evolved, in fact. These sea-dwellers had so far sufficed to keep the waters pure enough for life to subsist, being able to transform the poisonous salts which they assimilated as food, building calcium into their shells and bones. But now the situation has become critical, and new agents were needed.

We can imagine a committee of angels or *devas*, according to the religion we profess, older sons of God who direct earth's natural forces, sending forth a call for volunteers, and interviewing those creatures who responded with an offer of service. What a wonderful sight would have met their eyes when the Crinoids presented themselves! It was as if the bottom of the sea has become a forest of trees, with colourful branches waving like arms in the air, though there could have been no wind. We can imagine the Crinoids saying for themselves: "Look at us! We look like trees, but our trunks are made of stones among which we press our delicate bodies, so cementing them together as pillars; and we have branches, so that we can spread our arms to catch hold of the calcium that you want destroyed. It will serve us for food, and even when we die we shall not throw back the calcium, for we shall have consumed and transformed it."

Great numbers also came of humbler living things—not

of the Nautilus aristocracy or even the Crinoid—saying: "We have only simple forms, but you can rely on us to do the work." So both these offers were accepted, and these soldiers enlisted for the battle-front on the borders between land and sea. The tiny protozoa had a thirst so unquenchable that they could swallow incredible quantities of water-proportionately to their size it was as if a man should drink two cubic feet a second, without rest, for his whole life—and thus they filtered the water by passing it through their bodies, taking from it the salts to transform into their own structure, and giving back the water. Moreover, each one of them could produce in ten days a million reproductions of himself, so they made a formidable army of workers, and on dying each dropped its body as a solid particle of calcium, to add to earth round the coast-line.

It hardly agrees with the old-fashioned ideas of evolution that these simple forms should have displaced the far more complex Trilobites, but the cosmic plan had first consideration, and these creatures were content to serve it, regardless of their own progress. The proud Trilobites moves about awhile in massive elegance, but soon disappeared as no longer useful.

Ages passed and earth continued to rise from the waters and dry herself. New continents had been formed, new rivers drained them, carrying yet greater quantities of carbonate of calcium into the sea. The Crinoids were no longer able to work fast enough to maintain the equilibrium, and the crisis was met by another call for volunteers. This time the Coral Polyps answered it: "We look like stones, but we live and grow; and we shall stick together and drink, multiplying ourselves and building endlessly. We can build chains of mountains under the sea, cemented by our forms. We have our aviators too, who carry our spores to plant them in suitable places for our colonisation. But we demand good living conditions, away from the disturbed waters of rivermouths, and we must have our food brought to us, without having to go out and seek it for ourselves."

The tribunal of nature approved these reasonable terms, accepted the offer, and the Crinoids waved their arms in farewell, their task being done. So corals took over the important work of keeping the necessary equilibrium in the waters of ocean, and they have done it ever since without change or rebellion.

Who then could be used to bring food to these fixed workers, who had to stick to their jobs? Someone must stir currents round them, and for this task came fishes with fins, armoured and highly complex, hunting food for themselves and incidentally stirring the waters and bringing the corals what they needed. Later came unarmoured fish as well, lighter and quicker. These had soft spines without calcium, two double muscles and two fins to their tails, making them very fast, and mass production made up for their small size and defencelessness, since each individual could lay a million eggs. The problem of feeding them was solved by some eating others, all being given powers of speedy flight from greedy pursuers, so throwing the water into needed commotion. Does it seem to us cruel that they should be made to be eaten? We have to face the fact that the cosmic plan needs sacrifice, but just as such sacrifice is joyfully made by men when they offer their lives for their country, so animals find joy in fulfilling nature's purpose, though unconscious of any nobility.

If asked whether I agree with the theory of evolution, I answer that agreement or disagreement is a matter of no importance. We must look at facts to correct errors in existing theories, and thus add to knowledge, and I accept the geologist's view of evolution now as an advance on the biologist's, which formerly held the field. Geology furnishes the best proof of evolution, showing invertebrate sea-creatures followed by vertebrate, cold-blooded amphibians on land followed by warm-blooded animals and birds. Remains found in rocks allow the imagination to reconstruct past times, and realise an almost incredible age for our earth. A million years becomes the unit, and twenty-five million years a mere episode of world history. Such studies as geology and astronomy help us to conceive an eternity within infinity. They are the most fascinating subjects of our day, and children can and do feel their fascination.

The difference between the geological and biological views of evolution is that the latter considers life independent of the earth, another order of creation, put there to evolve—to live and grow towards perfection. It is a lineal view, akin to the old idea of the earth as a flat surface, suggesting that one who travelled on it indefinitely in a straight line must somewhere fall off the edge into space. Now we know that the earth is a sphere, and that this imaginary traveller need never cease going forward. So also the geological view of evolution shows us life of more dimensions, one with the earth and evolving with and through it, contributing to its upkeep and welfare. Biologists themselves have had to admit some failures in their theories, some creatures who unaccountably seem not to have had strength to evolve, and have remained static, with no brains to think with, no mouth even to eat with, no nerves to feel with. Such things as mollusca, for instance, they look on as evolutionary failures, but now have to admit their value as workers of the sea, preserving its purity. Plant life and animal alike now have to be considered from two points of view, and the more important is that of their function in the cosmic plan, which may require of them the sacrifice of long endurance of a static equilibrium, showing no development towards a greater perfection.

One side of evolution deals with the satisfaction of vital needs, defence, survival of the species and growth by modifications towards perfection. Another—and stronger—factor in evolutionary processes is concerned with the cosmic function of each living being, and even of inanimate natural objects, working in collaboration for the fulfilment of the purpose of life. All creatures work consciously for themselves, but the real purpose of their existence remains unconscious, yet claiming obedience. A coral polyp, if capable of conscious expression, would choose to live in calm and warm seas, undisturbed by river currents, and to have faithful attendants to bring it food without its having to stir in search of it. Corals never become aware that by their mode of living they preserve the purity of the water, so helping innumerable millions to live, and also build new land, to support future races. So the trees and plants might consciously exalt their desire for sunshine and vital need of carbon dioxide for their nourishment, unconscious that nature had given them these instinctual urges for the purpose of preserving the purity of the air, on which depended all higher life on earth. The bee who robs the flower of its nectar is aware only of his own need or the hive's, not that the flower's need of his visit is as great for its purpose of reproduction, for perpetuating the life of the species.

Man too, like all beings, has two purposes, conscious and unconscious. He is conscious of his own intellectual and physical needs, and of the claims on him of society and civilisation. He believes in fighting for himself, his family and nation, but has yet to become, conscious of his far deeper responsibilities to a cosmic task, his collaboration with others in work for his environment, for the whole universe, which truly, as the Bible says, "Groaneth and travaileth together," towards creative fulfilment. Victory in self-fulfilment can only come to the all, and to secure it some are content to sacrifice their own progress towards perfection of form, remaining inferior and humble workers like the corals, of static usefulness. Other species, having unconsciously reached their limit of usefulness and being unable to adapt themselves to conditions making new demands on them, disappear from the ranks of life, in which only the obedient and disciplined will continue to march, to the joyful music of the song of life.

6

How Mother Earth Has Been Created

To form an idea of the economy of our cosmic household it is of help to go back much further in geological epochs than the dawn of life, for great have been the changes and transformations that earth has undergone from even earlier times. Seashells are now found imbedded in the substance of rocks forming the summits of high mountains, and marbles, quarried in the middle of continents, prove to be made of highly compressed and polished calcareous matter, the remains of creatures whose very shape is traceable in the delicate patterns of the stone. As the sea creatures could hardly have journeyed to these inaccessible parts from their present watery depths and thence returned, the conclusion is reached that these mountains and inland plains must once have been under the sea, where these creatures lived and worked to elevate the land. How great must have been that deluge, of which there are so many mythical legends beside the one in the Bible! Coloured marbles are really corals, and still the same builders carry on their work, raising islands which will some day form a new continent in the Pacific. A new Asia is in the course of building while the old one slowly disintegrates.

Continents dissolve into the sea, and seas yield to growing land. Under our eyes everything is being worn down, to be rebuilt in new form. Who are the furniture-removers of the world? Who have decorated the original molten rocks with deposits that take the form of fantastic stalagmites and stalactites in caverns, snow-white towers and pinnacles of glittering salt, and tufaceous formations of marvellous colours in volcanic regions?

The toiler for all this beauty and treasure has been water, melting rocky substances and carrying them underground in solution, to bring them to the surface eventually by springs for the enrichment of earth's surface. Water is no thief, but gives back whatever it has gathered; always in passage from a place of high pressure, to one of low pressure it begins to fill each void by distillation. Drop by drop it leaves behind the load it was carrying, and gradually a pillar like an icicle hangs from the roof of the cave, towards another pillar that rises from the ground to meet it, made of particles of calcium left there by the falling drops. These majestic pillars soon fill the cave, making it a palace of beauty. Other minerals sometimes lend colour to the architecture—red, blue, pink and yellow—as veils and drapings of dazzling radiance. Such is alabaster of different colours, much found in Italy and prized by sculptors. Water is the great builder, creating and transforming. It hurries in love to the ocean bearing gifts, purifies itself, floats to heaven in its lightest form, to return as rain and begin work again.

Water is the great dissolvent, able to dissolve even iron. Not only is it able to do so, but it must, for it is the law of its being. Another power with which it is endowed is an indomitable energy. Always in motion, penetrating every hole and crevice, it flies to the skies as vapour to return as rain. Great as is its power, it works all the better as a dissolvent if helped by carbon dioxide, so this poison is also a natural agent, and a friend to water with which it works in association. The falling rain eagerly takes from the air its carbon dioxide, so air is usefully cleared of its poison, and water charged with the energy that will help it to dissolve the rocks. So charged, is a great miner, going deeper under earth's crust than any man can mine, to bring into circulation earth's buried treasure, for the fulfilment of the cosmic plan. The deeper it goes, the greater is the pressure, and the more is the water saturated with carbon dioxide, till supersaturated it gushes forth in a spring depositing the wealth it has gathered on its underground journey. By geysers and hot springs, as well as by volcanic eruptions, mineral wealth is brought to the surface.

Imagination can thus picture for us the primeval earth of hard, brown rock, unrelieved by verdure of grass of leaf, without sound of bird a living creature, the silence broken alone by plunging waterfalls, booming thunder or stones dislodged in avalanches. The grim brown crust is slowly being modified and overlaid with hospitable coverings, but before it can become the home of living beings some agency must ensure the purity of the air they will have to breathe.

Air is the natural environment of the animal, as water is of the fish; to be deprived of air to breathe is a more terrible fate than lack of food or water, and this necessary air is a delicate compound of oxygen and nitrogen in fixed proportions, with a minute quantity of carbon dioxide in it. A slight increase in the last ingredient makes air unbreathable bringing death by asphyxia, and on primeval earth the poisonous fumes must have been ever present, spued by geysers and craters from chaotic depths. The ratio of carbon dioxide in breathable air is only three parts in 10,000; how was that delicate balance achieved and maintained, that life might play its part in the future creation of the world? Surely there is a need here again to postulate a governing intelligence. The inanimate creation is accomplished, the stages have been reached when nature has to clothe the rocks and fertilise the soil, to make a living world. Again in imagination we hear an appeal that is also a command: "Come, O plants, upon the desert; live in it and transform it to beauty, and adjust the conditions you find in it to the needs of creatures who will follow you. Invade earth's farthest corners, and do your work." The plant life that was already established in the ocean heard the call and took the necessary leap to land. It was emphatically not to better their conditions, for those were already ideally suited to their living needs, and would long be far from being so on land. Yet on every shore, of sea, lake and river, the leap was taken, and the invasion began that would make the wilderness blossom as the rose.

For the task which they had undertaken, these new recruits had to be equipped, and so the sun, the mighty god of their adoration, gave them the rich gift of green colour, chlorophyll that would make them greedily devour the carbon dioxide that they found in the air, leaving the oxygen. Wherever verdure spread, the air was thus purified, and in due time the world was ready for animal life to start its evolutionary climb, the urge of life towards perfection and efficiency of service.

The evolution of the plants of earth is estimated to have taken about 300,000,000 years, from algae, mosses and lichens, through ferns to ever more complex forms of strength and beauty. Vegetation has accomplished its adventure with joy, conquering the earth, aspiring to the heavens, gripping the soil with strong roots to support noble pillars, roofed with interlacing branches and leaves opening millions of hungry mouths in the sunshine for carbon dioxide. In living and growing to perfection they thus did their cosmic task, and accomplished a further one in death, for dead vegetation was transformed into earth's inexhaustible supplies of coal. What could the men of our own day have accomplished without that coal, stored for him?

For many long ages plant life ruled the earth, the only animals being insects, crawling and flying, some of monstrous size. The ground was muddy and hot, and there were no seasonal changes as yet, the axis of the earth not having its present tilt to the plane of its orbit round the sun. The land was slowly sinking in parts, as it is even now, so forests became swampy that had been dry, and river waters filtered through roots that impeded their course, building with their deposits ramparts round coasts, till sediments covered old roots, new levels were maintained and soil laid in strata. There are places where a hundred forests are found to have been buried, one over another, showing how long was the period of sinking. The buried vegetation fermented, giving out gases, to become first peat, as found in the bogs of Ireland and the Netherlands. Under further pressure the peat gives way to lignite, then lithanthrax and lastly coal, destined to form the motor power for our industrialised civilisation. In the United States of America there is coal forty feet deep, stretching over a surface of one hundred and forty square miles, in one field alone. All this treasure of coal was given to earth in the Carboniferous Period by the sinking of forested lands. The Arctic lands, as Alaska and Siberia, are almost entirely made of coal, so must have had great forests and tropical climate.

Another humble worker in the earth's laboratory was the ferruginous microbe, who built its shell of the iron brought in solution by water from the interior of earth, and left its remains on death among the putrifying forms of plant life.

Wherever there is fermentation and stagnant water, brown patches may be seen, showing the ferruginous microbe still at work, as it was when iron deposits were laid side by side with coal, to the great convenience of modern manufacturers. These same microbes also produced an oily substance now yielding for us petrol.

Is it too much to say that we owe all our modern wealth and efficiency to the plants and creatures on sea and land who hoarded for us in life and death, that we also might live, breathe and work, continuing to fulfil the divine mandate: "Be fruitful and multiply, and replenish the earth!"

One epoch has closed in our review of creation, its last chapter being the invasion of land by the colonising plants. Nature led these plants to their adventure, to exert prodigious efforts and to triumph, only to be finally buried underground and carbonised. Have we to conclude that nature is cruel in carrying out the cosmic plan? Not so! In giving them an essential task to perform in her household economy, she gave that duty the form to them of satisfaction of a desire that could not be thwarted, a joy and no painful sacrifice. Life alone can say: "In my service is perfect freedom!" Work as the cosmic expression is ever a necessity of life and a joy; its shirking means extinction, the doom of original disobedience.

7

A Primeval World War

After many millennia of gradual and peaceful transformations on the surface of the earth, of balance being maintained between land and sea by many agencies, and of soil being enriched and mineral wealth deposited for future generations, we can imagine a critical point being reached when the earth grew impatient and rebelled. She would no longer stand the incroachments of water, but would prepare defences that would hold the enemy at bay. All round her coasts volcanic mountains belched fire, and hurled masses of molten rock and boiling mud, forming barrier-ranges in Asia, North Europe and Africa, the Rockies and Andes in North and South America. That was indeed a titanic world war, lasting millions of years, spreading to Australia, the East Indies and the Philippines, raising huge barriers that the water could not cross, so that parts of the sea got cut-off, to become lakes of which the water would evaporate, leaving desert sands. It would seem too as if at that time the sun's heat had diminished, or earth could not receive it in the former measure, for ice and glaciers, spread everywhere, only the equatorial regions remaining warm. Colossal salt deposits, even on mountain-tops where they form dazzling pinnacles today, are among the results of this war of the giants.

Was the elimination from the ocean of superfluous salt,

that must at this time have been endangering marine life, one reason for the great conflict that our imagination reconstructs? Certainly in the Permean Epoch had arisen an urgent necessity to reduce the salinity of sea water, and it could not have been done by living creatures forming shells of sodium chloride, as had been done with superfluous calcium carbonate. So the water had to be trapped on land, as if a cosmic cook had ladled out the soup that was too salty, replacing it with water. A cook who thus modified the flavour of some mixture would assuredly not waste the liquid he withdrew, and similarly the sea water that was cut off in great salt lakes was only stored for future use, the water evaporating to the clouds, to be later restored to the earth and through streams to the sea, and the salt to be left as rich deposits for man's use in due time.

Statistics show that men use one thousand million tons of salt a year, and men have been consuming salt for untold ages, so vast deposits have been needed. There are salt mines one hundred metres deep, magnificent palaces of crystallised salt, immense domes supported by pillars that flash like diamonds, reflected in calm lakes on the cavern floor. One such lies between Austria and Bavaria, near the notorious Berchtesgaden. It has been mined for twelve hundred years, and is in no danger yet of exhaustion, for there is a chain of such salt mountains, springing from a depth of five thousand feet below the ground. In Sicily a salt zone covers 2,400 square miles, and in Poland another covers 33,000 square miles, and is one hundred metres in depth. Asia Minor, Roumania, Persia, India have their saliferous mountains, and South America has a chain of them, the peaks being cones and pyramids of salt, shining like diamonds in the sun. In Tibet and the Hindu Kush, as in Abyssinia, are great deposits, proofs of inland seas that have evaporated on those high elevations, further proofs being the fossilised remains of marine creatures found in the rocks.

The uplift of these mighty ramparts was the achievement of earth in her rage, in a mood of fiery emotion; but still, in her more peaceful mood, the work goes on by which equilibrium is maintained, earth compensated for losses by erosion and sinking, and the sea rid of surplus salt. It may be seen going on in the salt lakes bordering the Red Sea, in deltas, where rivers are forced to find new outlets because of barriers raised against them, in the lagoons of the Mississippi and at Odessa. The Mediterranean would be a lagoon, but for the depth of the Straits of Gibraltar. In the Great Salt Lake of America none but a certain species of crustacean can live, and the Dead Sea is another well-known example of a portion of the sea left to evaporate to salt.

The titanic conflict which so altered the face of earth, and left stranded great portions of ocean, ended the period called Protozoic, and geologists call the succeeding period Mezozoic, to last one hundred and fifty million years. At its beginning, reptiles were kings on land, having developed from the first amphibians, creatures who could live in water or on land, but still laid their eggs in the water, as do frogs to this day. The first sub-period of the Mezozoic, called the Triassic period, saw the greatest amphibians, especially a sort of toad, which left its footprints in the sands of river-mouths, to be filled with sediment and remain impressed on rocks found today. It was huge in size and very clumsy, using its short legs more as oars than as limbs to carry its bulky body. It made great efforts to evolve better legs, and some at last succeeded in walking, the feet having three toes, so that its footprints were at first taken to be those of birds, till skeletons were also found. Some felt an urge to penetrate further inland by wriggling the body, instead of developing legs, so producing reptilean forms, some of which had sails on their back, perhaps at first to help them walk. Fossilised remains of these 'sails' show broken bones, as if they had proved more an obstacle than a help. They had teeth which were fitted to crush but not to grind. Reptiles still crush their food before swallowing, so differing from other animals. All these Triassic creatures ate enormously, eating trees with very tough leaves, and hard fruits like pine-cones, so needed very strong, flat-topped teeth. These animals were transforming the surface of the earth by their humus, which made the soil fit for finer kinds of vegetation.

In the next, or Jurassic sub-division of the Mezozoic period, came the reptiles of the Saurian family, like monstrous lizards, so heavy that they needed the support of water to hold them up, and spent most of their time in swamps. They had very small heads in proportion to the size of their bodies, and were slow-witted, sluggish creatures, always chewing. After the dinosaur came some slightly smaller saurians, who became carnivorous, now that flesh was more abundant. They could move much faster, walking on their hind legs, being able to stride twenty-one feet, and jump on their prey. They were very ferocious, and had teeth eight inches long. Some saurians developed the power to fly, being the original dragons of the old stories, and the Ptcrodactyl had wings that measured twenty to twenty-five feet across when spread. The wings were membraneous, each supported by an arm and one finger, while the other fingers remained as claws for perching, rather like bats of the present time. A few of these reptiles eventually grew tired of land residence, and went back to the sea, as the Ichthyosaurus, whose name means that it was half-lizard and half-fish.

Evolution could now accelerate its pace, and the stage was ready for higher forms of life to make their appearance.

8

The Cretaceous Period

This last sub-division of the Mezozoic takes its name from the clay and chalk deposits left by foraminifera, creatures living in the sea in vast numbers. The shells were round discs, made of eleven rings, and these were long after to be used by the Romans as money tokens. Radiolarians also appeared then, and a shell-fish called a Rodist, which was able to stand on feet and carry its shell, to retreat into it when danger threatened.

On land vegetation had evolved more deletate trees, with fan-like leaves, and the reptiles had armed themselves with hard, bony plates on backs and sides, some also having spines. One reptile had horns, two by its eyes and two by its nose, making a crown. Thus each was given by nature some protection from the carnivorous habits of neighbours, but no protection secured them from extinction at the end of the Mezozoic Age, when they had to give way to creatures much weaker than themselves, a proof in itself that 'The Survival of the Fittest' is no primary law of nature. It seems that the direct cause of their disappearance was that they took no care for succeeding generations, laying few eggs, and abadoning these few to be devoured by smaller creatures with more intelligence. The undefended young ones were a prey, because their parents did not stay by their side. So the stupid and lazy monsters no longer fulfilled any useful purpose, and the only way they could be used was as manure for the soil.

Glorious in its implications is the biological discovery that their evolutionary successors were the birds and mammals, weak of body but strong above all in motherly instincts, eager to defend their offspring to the death. If evolution meant just growth, how could sweet birds have come from ferocious monsters, joint heirs of their kingdom? But the instinct of protection for their offspring, which they as well as mammals reveal, is the true mark of evolutionary advance, rather than any gradual disappearance of teeth and growth of feathers. Nature evolved by strengthening what had been a weak point in animal behaviour, bestowing the new energy called love. This was to be a powerful passion as long as it dominated, able to make a small bird forget fear and care for self. Significantly it goes with warmth of blood. God's gift of love is powerfully revealed in mammals as well as in birds, and in it we recognise the secret of survival.

The only armoured reptiles which remain today are crocodiles and tortoises, and it is still the custom of turtles to hatch eggs in the sand, and abandon them for birds and animals to devour. Contrast this with the care shown by birds in hiding their nests in remote places, and guarding them from discovery; often they lure enemies away by exposing themselves to danger. Watch young birds being taught to fly, both parents in anxious attendance, entirely forgetful of self.

It was Fabre, the French naturalist, who brought to light this new idea in his book on *The Love of the Animals*, and *The Life of Insects*. Here was a scientist inspired to poetry, all by the magic of the one word "nest", with its tender associations. "But even more capable of love towards their offspring than the birds are the mammals, who protect them by allowing them to grow within their own bodies, and nourish them after birth with their own blood transformed to milk, besides caring for their helplessness at cost of great sacrifices. Birds and mammals are warm-blooded animals instead of cold, not like the reptiles, devoid of sentiment.

The first mammals to appear on earth were small and almost insignificant, yet they were destined to be kings of the next period of earth evolution. They became rapidly larger, and assumed the shapes that their bodies show today in the species that have survived. Horses of which fossilised remains have been found were of the size of a small dog. They had five toes on the foot, and lived in forests, eating trees. Later they learned to raise themselves on tip-toe, for speed in running, the knees of the hind-leg got to bend backwards instead of forwards, and toes that were not in use tended to disappear, the middle toe only remaining, while the rest joined the foot, as now in the horse and donkey.

Elephants also were small, rather like pigs with a long neck. Before the trunk appeared they had thirty-six teeth, of which two grew longer while ten were discarded by the time the nose had lengthened into a trunk. By that time it had yet reached the size only of a small mammal, truly a Lilliputian elephant.

The first camel to be traced was the size of a rabbit, but soon seems to have evolved to the size of a sheep. Its neck grew inordinately, like that of the giraffe, so that the fossilised remains were first named the camel-giraffe. It ate the leaves of trees, stretching its neck to reach them. Camels later took to dwelling in deserts, and so grew humps in which food and water could be stored.

The rhinoceros too was at first small, with a slender

shape and long, thin legs, able to run fast. It had bristly hairs to protect its skin from the flies. Kangaroos grew pouches for carrying their young, as they do still in Australia. A ferocious mammal was a sabre-toothed tiger, but most of them were vegetarian. A giant mammal then lived in the cold regions; its remains have been found preserved in ice, the flesh being still fresh enough for wolves and dogs to devour on extrication.

It was mammals such as these who developed into the forms of animals we know today, and among them, that which was to be assumed by man in the Cenozoic or Tertiary Period, from 580,000 BC. Scientists hesitate to include man entirely among animal life, and it is a fact that no direct link has been found, and that human remains have been found belonging to an earlier epoch than that of the larger monkeys who most resemble them.

Earth had now made herself ready for beings of more delicate needs, for her soil was rich in organic substances for their food, and grasses carpeted the ground for pasturage. New trees and plants had developed, propagating by seeds instead of by spores, and flowers were appearing, fit ornaments of the newly furnished house of life. It marks a climax in plant evolution when lichens, mossess and ferns gave way to flowering and seed-bearing plants. The help of the flying tribes for fertilisation was ensured by the adoption of attractive colours and scents, borne far by the helpful wind. There was endless variety, for different tastes had to be considered, and each flower had its special friend among the insects. The plant prepared the nectar, and the insect made himself more beautiful for invitation to the feast, the bee adding fur and velvet to his coat, and the butterfly shimmering with the gay hues on her wings. Collaboration was perfect between plants and creatures. The bees carried pollen on their furry bodies to fertilise the seeds of the flowers that they visited to collect their toll of wax and honey, so the needs of both were satisfied, and the deeper purposes of nature served.

Mild climates prevailed everywhere, magnolias and myrtles growing in regions now arctic. The earth must have been truly beautiful, and monsters in their gross stupidity and ugliness were unfit for it. Some tried "slimming", shortened their legs and managed to survive, especially those who had the intelligence to turn themselves into snakes. Those who were too lazy to make the effort to adapt themselves had just to perish. Snakes were the lineal descendants of dragons, and were not poisonous before the advent of man. They developed a double hinge to their jaw to enable them to swallow creatures of greater girth than their own, and they have always maintained a reputation for great cunning, or even wisdom.

9

The Earth in Travail Again

The earth is trembling with expectancy and glad foreboding. Her heart moved in sympathy with creation's joy; tremors ran through her frame and emotional tears coursed through her in new streams. Far different was her mood than when earlier, in the Permean Epoch, she had waged war on the encroaching waters. Now gentler and quieter, she was moved throughout her whole being to feel the near approach of man, her destined lord, and gifts were brought forth in new abundance for his use. Sympathetic warmth and love erupted in steady flow, in many parts of the world. All kinds of metal that earth had been preparing in her laboratories were brought to the surface and deposited, one being a shimmering substance that seemed like salt but was insoluble; this would later be supremely prized by men as diamonds. Of this largesse of mineral wealth, India received in rich measure, as the scene of earth's greatest emotion. If she does not today rank as the richest country, it is because her sons have still to release that wealth. If they do not do it themselves, others who toil and think more than they must inevitably take their place. Molten rocks on cooling crystallised in the forms not only of diamonds, but also of emeralds, sapphires and other precious stones. Amber developed from trees' resin in which insects had been caught and fossilised. The Greeks would later specially value amber, which they called Elektron, and deemed to have magic powers, to protect from the 'evil eye'. Many are earth's hidden and revealed treasures, of powers not yet all explored, hidden by nature not far from the surface, for men to seek and unearth. It was a child's curiosity that led to the first discovery of diamonds in Kimberley, resulting in the mines of South Africa. Will the day come when diamonds will be so plentiful that they will cease to be valued?

In earth's emotion, her crust wrinkled to form ridges in which again inland seas were enclosed, temperatures became more widely variable, sheltered valleys being warm, while ice and snow-covered mountain-tops, spreading in glaciers, by slow motion, to the plains. This ice-sheet soon pushed everywhere over earth's surface, grinding hill-tops and reducing them to dust; pushed even up-hill, it covered Europe, America and North India with an ice-sheet between one and two miles in depth. Surely a cold reception for man, a being without any covering of fur, in a glacial period that lasted many thousands of years. But there were some warmer valleys in which he could live, and the ice was itself a preparation for man's work, for it pulverised the rocks, leaving a soil of great fertility. Earth greeted her son with joy, but offered him toil, no enfeebling ease.

Though charts have been prepared extensively to enable the child to get some realisation of the nature and rates of living progress, it is not part of the Montessori method that he should be asked to memorise names or dates; he is merely to be interested in seeing how evolution has continually been accelerated in its processes. Seeds of interest have first to be sown in the child's mind—easily transplanted if first in the teacher's—and everyone must be ready for the full answering of his questions when he seeks further knowledge. Children like at first to place pictures separately prepared on blank charts, showing epochs only, and realisation is helped by the isolation of difficulties, one thing at a time being presented to their consideration, to avoid confusion. There is no interest for the child in a tangled skein of facts, to be memorised and recited in order. Some new educationists, in reaction from the latter, advocate giving him freedom to learn only what he likes, but with no previous preparation of interest. That is a plan for building without a basis, akin to the political methods that today offer freedom of speech and vote without education; the right to express thoughts where there are no thoughts to express, and no power of thinking. The necessity for the child, as for society, is help towards the building-up of mental faculties, interest being first of necessity enlisted, that there may be natural growth in freedom. My desire is to restore sight to the blind, that they may see for themselves, perhaps more than I am capable of seeing. Such is the love of a mother who helps her child to walk alone, though he may use his power to run from her.

Progress consists of achievement in less time. Children appreciate that by having to crowd more pictures on the later spaces of the chart. They see how brief has been the human span, compared with what went before it, yet how great has been its work. The child is allowed freely to build on this as on other points of interest, the material presenting the same facts, but from different angles. Engrams must be set to work, and given time, that consciousness may be clear. Some may not be interested at all, and others take more time or less to assimilate what they want. One thing has been well established by our experience, that facts are of less interest to the child than the way in which those facts have been discovered, and so children may be led to the history of human achievement, in which they want to take their part.

10

Early Man

Something new came into the world with man, a psychic energy of life, different from any that had yet been expressed. From the first he made use of tools, as no animals had done before, though some had hands with which they could pick things up. The first man whose traces have been found is called Palaeolithic meaning one who shaped tools of stone, and though very few of his remains have been found, his presence has been proved by discovery of his stone implements, of pointed and polished flint. It is significant that man should leave behind him his handiwork, traces of his creative intelligence, instead of his bodily remains among those of the lesser animals. Here is the colossal difference in this new cosmic energy. From those of the crudest type, soon man's weapons and tools became more finely worked and even began to show attempts at ornamentation, and he could scratch pictures on rocks.

The Palaeolithic Period is divided into Primitive, or of inferior work, and Secondary, with finer work in stone, when also traces of men's existence became more numerous and widespread. The Primitive sub-period is also known to scientists as Chellean, and those who study racial groups have come to the conclusion that there are still as many as twenty groups surviving on the globe which are at that stage of civilisation, though living under domination of a superior one. They are left as monuments of the far-distant past, and together with the traces found by geologists and archaelogists, and traditions handed down in literature during the last five thousand years, they enable us to see human life as a moving picture.

Each succeeding civilisation from the first has accelerated its pace, having more demands made on it. Not that the prime purpose has been to make life easier and happier for the individual, but rather that the environment made even greater claims on his service with each successive step, and men could only themselves evolve with their environment and through service to it. Even with an advanced civilisation, to stand still has ever been to stagnate and die.

Man is relatively of limited strength, with naked skin, weaponless and at a disadvantage physically to many other mammals, but he is given intelligence in rich measure, because he is destined to accomplish an essential work of creation, more than any other expression of life that has evolved. His new weapon was the mental one.

See him moving among ferocious beasts, with claws and teeth that rend, helpless too against barriers of mountains that barred exploit and adventure, envying the bird his wings that cleave the sky, the fish his power to swim. He could neither soar nor swim by nature; neither tear his enemies to pieces nor run fast from them. But the new weapon has proved to surpass all in effectiveness, and in time superiority in all has come, not to the more powerful arms and legs, but to the greater brain, and above all to imagination. Man is God's chief agent on earth for creation, not come merely to be its lord and enjoy himself, to be proud and boast as do the foolish. A man who triumphs in his superiority and in that of his race is never left to triumph long; he falls, leaving murder and destruction in his wake, as history abundantly proves. The truly great are humble. But we may legitimately be proud and rejoice that man has transformed his world in the long course of ages to one that is now beyond nature's contriving. Finding conditions worse when he came than any imagined for a Robinson Crusoe, man has built civilisation.

There were three glacial periods, with intervals between, the first and second being longer in duration, and reaching further south. Not long before man's arrival the Himalayas and the Alps raised their heads, and the Pacific Ocean was formed, where great masses of land had been submerged. Regions that were joined before became isolated. England and Ireland were for long in 'cold storage', and the Sahara was a pleasant and fertile country.

In the third Glacial Period earth was again covered with ice, but less far south. Between the Alps and the Caucasus stretched a temperate corridor where men dwelt. About 18,000 years BC the ice disappeared, and waterfalls poured such volumes into the ocean that there was another great flood, perhaps the original of the Biblical story.

Lands rose and sank, and out of the upheaval Italy took her present shape with Spain and Greece, the ocean being pushed inland to make the Mediterranean Sea of what had been a river before. Another river became the Red Sea, and there were many changes further west. Earth was calm once more, and could proceed to make her toilet.

During these troubled ages men had lived between ice-sheets, mostly in forests and by streams, in the neighbourhood of giant mammoths, sabre-toothed tigers, moose and deer, as well as small horses, a species of buffalo and giant beavers. There were no lions yet, or ordinary tigers, but elephants of small size made their appearance in the

Acheulian Period, that followed the Chellean. Then too came the muskox, antelope and sheep. These early men were giants, showing little intelligence as yet, though using rough tools. After 50,000 BC a smaller and cleverer race had appeared, using chips of stone as knives, and shaping them with some skill. Their food was berries, roots, snails, lizards, eggs and frogs; indeed they were omnivorous. They had strange funeral rites, and worshipped the dead. The Cromagnon man was rather like the American Indian. During the third Glacial Period animals and men alike lived in caves for shelter, and one dangerous neighbour was the Great Cave Bear. As the ice retreated, men and animals pressed into the forests, and men lived by hunting. Art made its appearance, statues being made, and heads of horses and other animals sculptured on rocks. Necklaces and other ornaments, with weapons and household implements, began to be buried with the dead, often found in a sitting position, with knees updrawn to the chin.

Migratory people came north from Africa, bringing lions, and west from Asia, bringing large horses, and by the time the Magdalaneans arrived man was no longer primitive, but worked on bones and horns instead of stone, used bone needles for stitching, and harpoons and javelins for fishing. These harpoons are still held by the superstitious to bring luck, and it is curious that they are found in Spain near the Pyrenees, where there is no evidence of water having existed at the time they must have come into use. The conclusion is that they were transported, and that already there was a trade in such articles of luxury and artistic beauty, for they were beautifully ornamented, especially those made in Egypt. As usual, it was the useless things, satisfying man's spiritual and aesthetic needs rather than utilitarian, that were bartered, men adventuring their lives to bring them.

Homo Sapiens had arrived, and after the disturbances accompanying the Great Deluge—or the last of them if more than one—had subsided, he was able to cultivate the richly fertile soil, domesticating animals to serve him and keeping dogs to guard them. He was master of all, dressing in skins or woven cloth from sheep's wool, with bow and arrows for weapons as well as knife, using ornaments of jade, gold and bronze, and artistic pottery for domestic purposes. This was an advanced civilisation, and man could henceforth be classified in two types, the shepherd and the cultivator, who would oppose each other through many ages.

11

Nomad versus Settler

From the beginning man was a hunter, needing to defend himself against ferocious creatures of superior strength, and later wanting to kill for food, as his tastes grew more carnivorous and he grew more confident in his cunning. After a time he learnt to domesticate some of the animals, for his use and convenience. It was not done, as usually assumed, by taming them, but by capturing and keeping them in captivity. Captive animals who were able to adapt themselves and bear young in the conditions provided by man naturally became domesticated, while others, as antelopes and zebras, never so adapted themselves. In Egypt lions, hyenas and leopards were commonly kept in captivity. It seems likely that at first domestication was for sacred purposes rather than domestic, cattle being chosen for sacrifice because of their horns, and milk being first drunk by the priests, later by other people. The cow remains sacred in India, and all religions have relics of sacred animals. About fifty species in all out of a hundred thousand species of wild animals have been domesticated by man.

Two instincts may be found in man, one being that of wandering, and the other its opposite, of attachment to a spot. The former was earlier to be expressed, and as men gathered flocks and herds of domestic animals, there was the need to be continually on the move, to find fresh pasturage when one was exhausted. But soon settlers were to be found, in contrast with these nomads. After men had remained long enough in one spot to effect some transformation of it, they formed an attachment to it and stayed there, cultivating the ground for crops and forming a community. Such settlements were usually at river mouths, or in well-watered and fertile tracts of country.

Settlers produce, and nomads come to take the fruits of their labour, generally by force of arms. Such seems to have been the course of history from the earliest time, and though apparently unjust, it has helped, by mixing productions and cultures, to develop civilisation. It has been in spite of themselves that men have been brought together and organised, for each group has ever grown in conscious exclusiveness and prejudice. The common language would unite the group, tending to become more complicated with advance in civilisation, and a particular religious system would be formed from traditions and customs, especially with regard to the disposal of the bodies of the dead. Every settlement would have its taboos against alien habits of food and clothing, and priests tended to oppose innovation and guard against any relaxation of exclusiveness. In fertile river basins and on deltas, art and literature developed and all sorts of industries, music and the means of spiritual satisfaction, but the individual became rather lazy and selfish, his psychology being directed to getting the maximum result from the minimum effort. Nomadic people would visit these settlements, sometimes acting as traders between one centre and another of civilisation, and would be envious of the conditions they found, themselves strong enough to seize for themselves, though deemed inferior.

Civilisation is to be judged not only by its outer

appearance, but also by its moral standards. Nomads did not evolve outwardly so much as the settlers, and were usually despised as barbarians, but they developed certain qualities which were far in advance of those who scorned them. Their mode of life required of them great discipline, order and bravery, endurance of cold, heat, lack of food and water, and a special tribe loyalty and devotion to a leader. Such qualities gave them easy victory over the softer communities, and so the plan has inevitably been fulfilled, racial and tribal cultures mixing, all human wealth in constant circulation. The products of civilisation soon superimposed themselves on barbaric conquerors, who in turn adopted settled habits and softened. Things which were an improvement on what had gone before could never be lost or discarded.

Except among primitive tribes villagers no longer arm themselves against raiders and unwelcome strangers, but still nations arm themselves to defend their borders, and recognise duties only to their own people, ignoring human unity, or just beginning to give it a grudging recognition. So it has been necessary hitherto for violence to bring about mixtures; wars and conquests, migrations of surplus population for colonisation, trade, exploitation of mineral wealth, and mere love of adventure and change, which still makes some people restless seekers after danger, challengers of obstacles. Stagnation has meant death, so people have never been left to stagnate for long, and conquests have resulted finally in added wealth of one kind or another to both conquered and the conqueror, and to the sum of human life in general.

If human unity—which is a fact in nature—is going at last to be organised, it will be done only by an education that will give appreciation of all that has been done by human cooperation, and readiness to shed prejudices in the interests of common work for the cosmic plan, which may also be called the Will of God, actively expressed in His entire creation. We hear much talk, largely ineffective, of world-organisation but the word that should be used is rather 'Organism'. When it is recognised that the world is already a living organism, its vital functions may be less impeded in their operation, and it may consciously enter on its heritage in the day towards which hitherto "all creation has been groaning and travailing together."

Religions and languages keep men apart, while arts, sciences and products of industry unite them. Where there is fixation of spirit to an idea, it is difficult to change, and a language cannot easily be transmitted because it is incarnated. By their language people of a group become in tune with each other, but others cannot tune in to them. It seems an impasse that must continue to baffle us, since regional languages are everywhere being revived and defended with fierce vigour, and religions show little tendency yet to federate, while the thoughtful see yet more danger in deliberately cultivating the irreligious spirit.

The answer to all the contradictions lies in right education, and results can be achieved in no other way, political or social. It requires the influence of sacred and deep things to move the spirit, and the new children of civilised humanity must be given a profound emotion and enthusiasm for the holy cause of humanity. Religion then will not need to be taught, which indeed it cannot really be, but reverence for truth, inner as well as outer, will grow in natural freedom, and the barriers of language will be allowed to give way before economic forces arrayed against them, when better mutual understanding of human purposes prevails.

12

Man: The Creator and Revealer

Imaginative reconstructions of the past history of our globe and its living inhabitants have been made passible to us only by the discoveries of intelligent men. They have been the result, not of common intelligence unaided, but with the help of systematic science. The man of culture today is superior to the natural man, having sensorial powers far beyond those given by nature, through the telescope and microscope which extend his vision and through the accumulated researches of mathematicians, chemists and physicists who have investigated the secrets of nature, by the magical powers of the human mind. So appears the greatness of man, a creative agent and transformer above animals or plants, explorer of the whole world and the universe outside it, able even to go back in time, and explore what has long ceased to be.

Every subject of our interest and study can be related to human beings, who have toiled, often starved, to overcome obstacles for its understanding, and to give us knowledge free of such pains. Everything is the fruit of a human soul, and we incarnate this fruitage in education, this treasury of riches handed on to us by man. We must ourselves feel—and inspire in the children—admiration for all pioneers, known and unknown, possessors of the flame which has lighted the path of humanity.

Most people are slow to interest themselves in new things; even the intellectual people make hardly any progress in the world of thought, looking with hostility on any new idea that challenges mutual security. Mentally as well as physically people are lazy, wanting only to enjoy life. The more then is admiration due to those who are different, urged by an inner force to do things even against their own welfare and happiness, to the extent of endangering their lives.

The Greeks, more than two thousand years ago, had achieved great things in art and literature, and were highly cultured for their age. One Greek who was a poet did not feel able to accept as true all the things that he was told of barbarian folk outside Greece, as that people of the north slept six months of the year, and those of the extreme south were all baldheaded. He decided to travel and see for himself if these things were true. He was warned of many dangers, of man-eating giants and sorcerers, as well as perils of unknown oceans and elemental forces. But he persisted; he must travel to fulfil his life. He went off in a small ship, slowly propelled by oars and sail, and his friends thought never to see him again. But after seventeen years he returned, and his old friends eagerly gathered round him to ask him questions. Had he seen a Cyclops—a giant with one eye in the middle of the forehead or a man who slept for six months at a stretch? What about centaurs and mermaids? He answered that he had seen not these but greater wonders, men much like himself in all countries, eating and sleeping and dressing much as he did; Babylon a marvellous city, with houses three storeys, high and hanging gardens, perfumed ladies and wise philosophers; Persia, where they worshipped one god instead of many, kissed each other on meeting in the street, and educated children to read, shoot arrows, and always to speak the truth.

The returned traveller, whose name was Herodotus, wrote all these things and many others in a book to read to his friends, and is now called 'the Father of History', for this book was the first of its kind.

Alexander the Great, another Greek, was also a great traveller, founding Alexandria in Egypt, and many other towns named after him. Alexandria became the home of a great university, and its director was also a discoverer, though of a different kind. He wanted to explore mentally, to throw new light on mathematics and astronomy. From observations of the earth's shadow on the moon in eclipses he discovered the earth to be a sphere. He divided a circle into 360 parts and calculated earth-measurements. He found that when the sun was directly overhead at Assouan, on the same meridian as Alexandria, it made an angle with the zenith of 7 degrees, and as the distance of Assouan from Alexandria by actual measurement was 5,000 stadia, by proportion he could calculate the circumference of the earth. This Greek was called Eratosthenes, and he lived about the year 200 BC. Also in 200 BC an Egyptian called Ptolemy made a map of all known countries of the world, showing on it a great part of Asia, and Africa, as well as the Mediterranean countries of Europe.

We still have discoverers of this kind among us. Only twenty-five years ago the President of the Natural History Museum at New York was convinced that the Gobi Desert in Central Asia would yield valuable results, if explored for remains of the earliest monsters. People laughed at him, and thought it a waste of money and toil, but he persisted and organised an expedition, Mr. Anderson, the Curator, himself going in charge, because he had previously conducted an expedition to study the life of whales in the Arctic Seas, and enjoyed such pioneering. With him went ten men who had faith in him and in the project. They reached Peking, and bought three cars, but still encountered nothing but discouragement, everyone warning them of terrific desert storms, excessive heat by day and cold by night, far from human aids or comforts. Besides, how could there be remains of amphibian reptiles on such an elevated plateau, far from any sea? But they went on, armed with rifles, joining other caravans at first, but soon left quite to themselves to penetrate the dread unknown of the interior. No one expected these crazy men would survive to return. Persevering amid untold difficulties they began digging in the sand, a dreary waste of seemingly endless extent and monotony. At last they suddenly saw a small piece of actual bone, and began to dance round it in delight, for it was the proof that their faith was justified. Before they returned they had found proof enough. A place where dinosaurs had lived and died in hundreds! They had solved a problem by the discovery of many eggs, proving how these reptiles propagated their young. In the course of digging they came across huge columns, looking like the bones of some monstrous mammal. Then other bones were found, evidently of the same creature, and lastly legs in a standing position, showing death by sinking in a quicksand.

So they had plenty wherewith to return to New York, and were well satisfied, though they gained no rewards for themselves. They had won a moral victory, and added to the sum of human knowledge, but many still thought them crazy, to dig in a desert and rejoice to find some old bones.

We do not cultivate admiration for these past and present adventurers and explorers for the sake of paying them with our gratitude, for they are beyond our reach; but we want to help the child to realise the part that humanity has played and still has to play, because such realisation leads to an uplift of soul and conscience. History must be alive and dynamic, awaking enthusiasm, destructive of intellectual egoism and selfish sloth. For two thousand years we have been taught: "Thou shalt love thy neighbour as thyself" and we are little nearer to the doing of it, for mere preaching does nothing. Loftiness of mind is usually taught through poetry and literature, expressions of the soul of man, intangible and almost meaningless to the child's mind. But the history of human achievements is real, a living witness to the greatness of man, and the children can easily be brought to thrill to the knowledge that there are millions of people like themselves, striving mentally and physically to solve the problems of life, and that all contribute to a solution though one may find it.

In the field of thought as in geological eras environment has to be prepared for an impending change. When the right preparation of thought is complete, discoveries may take place by the organisation of many minds in this suitable mental atmosphere. The crystallisation point of hundred of intellects is in the person of one man, who expressed something strikingly useful or discovers new knowldge. Except in poetry, pioneers, always depend on the help of those who have gone before them; the present stands on the past, as a house on its foundation. Man has gone far beyond nature in the work of creation, and he could not have done so unless he had accepted and felt a God with no hands or feet, who yet walks through the lengths and breadth of the universe, fashioned and still being wrought by Him, through human and other agents.

Man finds himself no longer limited to his hands for the accomplishment of his desires, for he has machines. Super-nature is now his desires, for he has machines. Super-nature is now his background of potentiality. A wider, loftier life is his than ever before, and children have to be prepared for it, so the fundamental principle in education is correlation of all subject, and their centralisation in the cosmic plan.

13

Early Great Civilisations

It is only recently that research in history has had the aid of science, and one consequence has been that hypothetical dates for the beginnings of social organisation have been pushed back, and cannot yet be fixed. It is astonishing to find that at no period of antiquity yet explored has mankind seemed without centres of civilisation of a relatively advanced type, however barbaric the huge majority, and scholars have now to admit a certain basis of truth to many traditions and myths formerly slighted.

Especially has a change of chronology become necessary with regard to eastern traditions. Civilisation had of late been regarded as mostly a Western product, linked only slightly with ancestral centres in the east. Indian sages have consistently claimed an antiquity for their records, and works of profound philosophy, which used to outrage the credulity of Western scholars, but which now has found sufficient corroboration to command respect if not yet entire acceptance. One fact clearly established is that Asiatic civilisations of advanced type far antedate European, and even Egyptian, and that both derived from a yet earlier land, a lost continent.

It has been shown in previous chapters how frequently the earth has undergone transformations, through natural agencies, in fulfilment of a plan. One such caused terrific floods to submerge an entire land under the waters of the Atlantic Ocean, about 75,000, BC. The only remnant left of this Atlantean continent was an island called Poseidonis, which in its turn sank in the tenth millennium BC, as historically recorded by the Greek sage, Solon, who had received the knowledge from the Egyptian priests. These world catastrophes, which so altered the face of the Western world, changed also parts of Asia, submerging most of old Lanka to the south of India, and raising the Himalayas and Central Asian plateau. But life was not interrupted and cut off in Asia as in Atlantis, and civilisations survived and specially flourished, fed by successive streams of Atlantean immigrants who had perhaps been led by portents and priestly warnings to flee from the doomed land, or had come in the usual course of colonisation. Atlanteans seem to have been known for an adventurous and colonising race, as well as of imperial wealth and power, and their culture long survived in Egypt and Peru as well as in many parts of Asia, where it may clearly be distinguished from that of succeeding Aryans.

The people who came to occupy the marshy lands of Europe as soon as they were sufficiently dry for habitation arrived in successive waves from Central Asia, some by way of the Caucasus and the Mediterranean coasts, and others by a more northern route, having left their Aryan cradle-land probably because it was drying up to an uncomfortable extent 20,000 BC, for the Gobi Desert is thought now to occupy that part of the earth's surface. Those who did not migrate to Europe or Africa trekked south into Persia and India, turning that land into Aryavarta as they gradually permeated or conquered the Atlantean states there, peopled by wealthy and sophisticated folk of an effete civilisation and somewhat evil habits—the *rakshasas* of old Indian tales.

So India became a great link between the most ancient

and later civilisations, making a somewhat uneasy whole through some irreconcilable differences, but developing rare tolerance and cohesive social structure through its great leaders, philosophers and saints. Scholars cannot yet agree just when the divine Sri Krishna drove the chariot of Arjuna on the field of Kurukshetra, or when the perfect king Rama fought Ravana to recover his beautiful wife, Sita, but few now deny these a place in history.

More fully attested are the records of Lord Gautama the Buddha, whose religious followers number the greatest among the faiths, and of the Hindu philosophers Sri Sankaracharya and Sri Ramanujacharya, who perhaps did as much to establish of Indian civilisation a spiritual keynote which no other land has approached. Isolated for many years from healthful outer contacts with other Aryan peoples, of late centuries conquerors and traders have made settlements within India's borders, to her ultimate benefit as well as their own, Muslims adding their culture to enrich the national pattern of life, and providing one of her wisest rulers in the person of the Mughal Emperor, Akbar. English rule since has brought the currents of modern western thought, and stirred political activity.

In the ancient world, the place of universities was taken by religious institutions called Mysteries, and which greatest men of intellect sought admission, and which had the truly international affiliations. The greatest of these were in India, Babylon and Egypt, the latter Greek mysteries of Eleusis and elsewhere being derivatives. The original centre was traditionally Atlantis, in its Golden Age of splendour and wisdom, and the Druids of Britain and Gaul too derived their knowledge from that source. The great Greek scholar Pythagoras travelled to Babylon and India to learn wisdom from the Magi and Brahmans.

Another Asiatic centre of civilisation from the earliest times is the great land of China–or–Cathay–now again being regenerated after many years of soulsearing conflict, and attracting more and more the attention of scholars, by its secret of eternal youth and beauty. Not much archaeological research has yet been done in China, no date can be fixed for its beginning, but it has had an advanced type of civilisation ever since anything of it has been known to other men. Its flaw has been that the Chinese were too satisfied with their own perfection of evolutionary development, and isolated themselves dangerously from outer contacts—as fatal a course to humans as we have seen it to be to animal species.

The people of China, Turanians and Mongolians alike, are thought to have come from Atlantean stock, and some connect them with the Akkads of Western Asia, displaced by Semites from the Mesopotamian lands. No one knows how long ago the Chinese developed the art of printing, and made other inventions, as the mariner's compass, which Europeans were to learn from them centuries later. Their great sage, Lao Tze, was the founder of Taoism, and was a contemporary of the Buddha, whose religion spread also to China, to harmonise and blend with it. But Chinese culture and manners owe yet more to the sage Confucius, born also in the sixth century BC, who wrote the chief Chinese classics, and still commands the veneration of all.

A Venetian traveller, called Marco Polo, made known to Europe in the thirteenth century the riches and power of the ancient empire, and since then many commodities and inventions have been borrowed, including printing, processes of silk production and choice teas, and gunpowder. Its doors have had to be forced open to commerce, and through many vicissitudes it has preserved its spiritual integrity.

14

Egypt Through the Ages

Egyptian civilisation seems to have flourished—with a few black-out periods—from the Palaeolithic Age to the present day, and to have given rise through the Greeks to most of the culture of Europe. From her central position and the wealth of her natural resources, owing to the bounties of her river, Egypt was fitted to be the point from which civilisation spread, and she had the further advantage of having inherited vast knowledge of science and art from the earlier people of the lost continent. Egyptians too had a genius for colonisation, being able to transfer their environment; they had creative minds, able to invent what others could copy.

A discovery of tremendous importance to humanity was made in Egypt, as usual the result of a series of partial discoveries that led up to it. The seasonal flooding of the Nile always left rich soil and sprouting vegetation in its wake, and the thought seems to have occurred to some farmer to dig channels for further conveyance of the life-giving streams. So irrigation began to be practised, and was copied by people living in similar river-basins, especially in Mesopotamia. Another Egyptian discovery was copper, of great importance. Green matter was deposited on the banks of the Nile, wherever water eddied in stagnant pools with many floating algae on the subsidence of floodwaters. Egyptians highly prized the colour green, which they looked on as life-giving, even painting their faces green to promote long life. Finding then this green Malachite, they ground it up to mix with fat for a skin-paste, and tried heating it over a fire for better mixing. The fat burnt out, and a hard deposit was left, which was copper. This new substance began to be used for beads, pots and ornaments, and it was made in large quantities. Vessels of chiselled copper were very costly, but were unbreakable, so in great demand, and mining was started to get more malachite. Brass too was soon worked, musical instruments being made of brass and strings. The Egyptians were master craftsmen, unsurpassed in their technique, and they loved their work. Even beds were far more beautiful than ours today; they had legs wonderfully carved to look like animals, and ornamented steps for climbing into them, but only a hard wooden head-rest for pillow. This was about 4,000 BC, and tables, chairs and mirrors were also then of marvellous beauty. Spoons were of inlaid ivory, and ladies used ornamental combs in their hair. Thus the Egyptian soul expressed itself in beauty. They had the custom of burying ornaments and musical instruments with corpses in the tombs, from where they have been recovered, and also agricultural implements, and statues of slaves, who were expected magically to become alive in the land of the dead, and then to till the lands of their lord as they had done on earth. Dead bodies were taken across the Nile in processions of three boats. One carried the priests and relatives with the sarcophagus or coffin; the second took professional mourners who were required for the rites, and the third was loaded with food and all the precious things to be interred for the use of the dead. On arrival at the other side of the river, the coffin would be drawn to the tomb by bulls or oxen, who would be sacrificed during the rites. Many inscriptions of sacred writings have been discovered on the walls of tombs, later written on rolls of papyri, and these have been collected in *The Book of the Dead*, which scholars have been able to decipher. This cult of the dead has been of great service to history, but it was not intended for that purpose, any more than plants intended to bury themselves to give us coal.

For the embalming of their dead the Egyptians needed many rare herbs and spices, besides precious stones and metals for ornamental work, and they used two different kinds of boats, one for the Nile and the other for the sea, with beautifully embroidered sails. In these boats they coasted the Mediterranean and Red Sea, and sailed down the East African coast as far as Somaliland; they penetrated the Persian Gulf to Syria and beyond, and were familiar with the island of the Aegean Sea and Asia Minor.

Sumerians were settlers on the shores of the Persian Gulf, and a legend tells of a great fish who came to them bringing gods who taught them many marvels, and departed again within the body of the fish. These Sumerian people also developed a fine civilisation, perhaps helped by the Egyptians. Some years ago great archaeological discoveries were made in Mohenjodaro, in north-west India, where Sumerian remains were found.

Egyptians paid other men to fight for them, and they made slaves work for them, so progress in civilisation does not always involve moral goodness. The Pyramids and other marvellous monuments were built by slaves, under cruel task-masters. A great Pharaoh arose who was a religious reformer, wanting to purify and simplify worship, saying that the most important duty was to live in the Truth and seek Truth. The priests were too strong for him to succeed, and he was dethroned, but Egypt was no longer united and began to decline.

Ancient religions are no longer able to be neglected or despised in the study of history, because they are an important part of human psychology. The most primitive men possess religious sensitivity, which makes them able to see spirits in the living and dead, in trees, sun and stars. They see them with the eye of imagination, with which we are able to pierce the mystery existing in nature. Man cannot do without his religion, which has suited each stage of his development. There were many deities in Egypt, and much mystery surrounding them, the chief of all being the sun, who created the world and man, leaving them in the care of Pharaoh, his son. The sun was called Amon-Ra, and none other equalled him, but lesser gods were many. Wonderful tales were told of Isis and Osiris, incarnated gods who ruled Egypt. Osiris was betrayed and killed by enemies, and Isis long sought to find his dismembered body, finally to recover it. Then Osiris became ruler of the dead, while Isis and her son Horus ruled earth. Man lived on earth under the eye of Ra, and then went to Osiris, to be judged, the heart being weighed in a balance against truth. The superstitious would fill the heart of a dead body with lead, that it might deceive Osiris with its weight in the judgment.

No comprehensive account of Egypt's history can be given here, but only a guide to necessary study. The philosophy of modern history lays emphasis on the meeting and mixing of people, groups with tendencies to merge into large groups, nations at last to start organising the unity of humanity. Mixing has ever been a slow process, and civilisation is its product. Teachers should study the origin, geographical position and growth of each group, its movements and relations with other groups, taking the life history of the whole people rather than individuals; such facts can be given to the children in an acceptable form.

15

Life in Babylon, and Her Dealings with Tyre

The land watered by the two rivers, the Euphrates and the Tigris, now called Mesopotamia, has been the scene of almost as ancient a civilisation as that of Egypt. They were long contemporaries and rivals, but Babylon had the more chequered career, often falling to conquerors, and archaeologists have found remains of many buried cities in the sands, as Nineveh, a neighbouring and senior capital to Babylon. Chaldaean, Assyrian, Babylonian and Persian empires held sway there in turn within a thousand year BC, for its borders were not well protected by nature.

Rawlinson in his *History of Babylon* describes the great city as it must have been in the days of Nebuchadnezzar the King, familiar to Christians through the pages of the Bible. It was full of people from all parts of the known world—dominant Semites with their long beards and flowing robes; clean-shaven Sumerians with short kilts. These Sumerians were people of an earlier civilisation who had been subjected, but who commanded the respect of their Semite conquerors for their learning. Many came to consult their wise men, who were soothsayers and astrologers. Temples were centres of city life, and priests were wealthy and powerful.

There was much less beauty of architecture than in

Egypt, streets being narrow, and buildings made of ugly brick, the colour of clay. Brass was used and pottery was not highly artistic. There were many canals, made by Hammurabi, the legendary founder, who had left to his people wise laws, giving special protection to women and to the poor. These laws and other writings are found written on bricks, which were used for books. A pointed instrument was used to scratch characters on the soft clay of the brick, which would then be baked in the sun to harden and preserve the writing. Thousands of these volumes have been unearthed; Nebuchadnezzar had a library full of them in his palace.

The Babylonians were a peaceful people, easily running away from the army of a conqueror, but soon returning to rebuild homes. At this time there were about seven million inhabitants, and the city was enclosed by a wall three hundred feet high, thick enough for a team of four horses to be driven abreast along its top. This wall was fifty miles long and had one hundred gates, the most beautiful one being dedicated to Ishtar, Goddess of Love and War. This gate had six towers of bronze and gold, inlaid with enamel.

A wonderful avenue led from the King's Palace to the Temple of Merodach; it was lined on either side with huge statues of bulls and lions, fashioned of metal and enamel. These statues may now be seen in the British Museum. Lions and Bulls are two of the Signs of the Zodiac, standing for the star-constellation still called Leo and Taurus. All ancient religions held these signs in great reverence.

Babylon traded not only with Egypt, but with the Phoenician city of Tyre, a maritime state whose people traded all round the coasts of Europe and Africa, as far even as the British Isles. A fine description of the splendours of Tyre is given by the Jewish prophet Ezekiel in the Bible, from reading which we can well imagine how people lived in Babylon and Egypt as well as in Tyre and her colonies. Ezekiel prophesies a great victory that Nebuchadnezzar of Babylon would win over Tyre:

> Now, thou son of man, take up a lamentation for Tyrus;
> And say unto Tyrus, O thou that art situated at the entrance of the sea, which art a merchant for the people of many isles, thus saith the Lord God; O Tyrus, thou hast said, I am of perfect beauty.
> Thy borders are in the midst of the seas thy builders have perfected thy beauty.
> They have made all thy ship-boards of firtrees of Senir; they have taken cedars from Lebanon to make masts for thee.
> Of the oaks of Bashan have they made thine oars; the company of the Ashurites have made thy benches of ivory, brought out of isles of Chittim.
> Fine lines with broidered work from Egypt was that which thou spreadest forth to be thy sail; blue and purple from the isles of Elishah was that which covered thee.
> The inhabitants of Zidon and Arvad were thy mariners; thy wise men, O Tyre, that were in thee, were thy pilots.
>
> *   *   *
>
> Tarshish was thy merchant, by reason of the multitude of all kind of riches; with silver, iron, tin and lead they traded in thy fairs. Javan, Tubal and Meshech, they were thy merchants; they traded the persons of man and vessels of brass in thy market.
> They of the house of Todarmah traded in thy fairs with horses, and horsemen and mules.
> The men of Dedan were thy merchants; many isles were the merchandise of thine hand; they brought thee for a present horns of ivory and ebony. Syria was thy merchant, by reason of the multitude of the wares of thy making; they occupied in thy fairs with emeralds, purple and broidered work, and fine lines, and coral, and agate. Judah and the

land of Israel, they were thy merchants; they traded in thy market wheat of Minnith, and Pannag, and honey, and oil, and balm. Damascus was thy merchant in the multitude of the wares of thy making, for the multitude of all riches; in the wine of Helbon, and white wool. Dan also and Javan going to and fro occupied in thy fairs; bright iron, cassia and calamus were in thy market.

Dedan was thy merchant in precious clothes for chariots.

Arabia and all the princes of Kedar, they occupied with thee in lambs, and rams, and goats; in these were they thy merchants.

The merchants of Sheba and Raamah, they were thy merchants; they occupied in thy fairs with chief of all spices, and with all precious stones and gold.

*   *   *

These were thy merchants in all sorts of things, in blue clothes and broidered work, and in chests of rich apparel, bound with cords, and made of cedar, among thy merchandise.

The ships of Tarshish did sing of thee in thy market; and thou wast replenished and made very glorious in the midst of the seas.

Such is the poet's description of wealthy Tyre, destined to humiliation by the yet mightier power of Babylon, then achieving world-empire. But another Jewish Prophet, called Jeremiah, was almost at the same time denouncing the wickedness of Babylon, and foretelling its doom:

Babylon hath been a golden cup in the Lord's hand that made all the earth drunken; the nations have drunken of her wine, therefore the nations are mad.

Babylon is suddenly fallen and destroyed; howl for her; take balm for her pain, if so be she may be healed.

Make bright the arrows, gather the shields; the Lord hath raised up the spirit of the kings of the Medes, for his device is against Babylon, to destroy it.

In other parts of the Bible is to be found the story of Nebuchadnezzar's doom of madness, and his son's fatal banquet when the fingers of a hand appeared writing on the wall that the kingdom was to be taken from him that very night. So actually was a surprise attack made on Babylon, and the empire passed to Darius the Mede and Cyrus the Persian.

These Medes and Persians were sterner and more virtuous people, of less civilisation, as having not long emerged from nomadic habits; they were destined to hand on the torch of civilisation to the Greeks in time.

16

Dignity and Impudence

From the cosmic point of view mixtures of civilisations are brought about for results that are wanted, much as in the culinary art. Different ingredients are separately prepared, carefully manipulated and patiently left perhaps to simmer gently till a desired condition is reached, before being added to the dish where the additional flavour is required. Thus in the Egyptian period events were few and took place slowly, civilisation spreading peacefully and many things being developed by degrees. The Babylonian civilisation then was added to it as a sort of sauce, having itself been flavoured with many early ingredients as well as some touch of Hittites and Scythians. Then came the Medes and still more Persians, and with these came a transformation in the dish. A chemical change seems to have taken the place of the mixture, and something that was not previously there.

The empire of Darius was very rich and magnificent, with palaces at Susa, Persepolis and Thebes of equal splendour, as if he had many capital cities. The Medes had been mountaineers, and the Persians of kindred origin, nomadic people like Scythians and Hittites, who under great leaders suddenly developed overwhelming strength and took the spoils of victory. They had great love of truth, and a especial reverence for law, so that it became proverbial that the law of the Medes and Persians was inviolable. Cyrus conquered not only Babylon but Egypt, establishing sway over all the lesser countries. Darius consolidated the empire, appointing satraps or governors to rule in his name and administer justice. He made good roads, linking India with Greece. Darius had great generosity, and he set the captive Jews whom he found in Babylon free to go back to Jerusalem and rebuild their temple which Nebuchadnezzar had destroyed.

The King's bed in Persepolis was wonderfully beautiful; its pergola was covered with a climbing vine of which the leaves and fruits were chiselled in gold. He had a bodyguard of ten thousand men, and he led a campaign against the Scythians, who lived in the mountains between the Caspian and the Black Sea, and whose strength and ferocity were fabulous. Darius did not believe what was told of these giants, that they had one eye only and goats' feet that enabled them to climb; so he invaded their country, and took it in four years, causing the Scythians to migrate north and west to the steppes. Many rock inscriptions have been found in different places commemorating the great deeds of Darius, King of Kings, as the one which Rawlinson found on a rocky ledge 3,000 feet high in mountainous country that he travelled through on his way to India in 1828. Even this mighty empire of Darius had soon crumbled away, for his own brave Medes and Persians were insufficient to hold together so vast an empire, depending for its defence on very heterogeneous hordes of men.

Darius, King of Kings, whose decrees went forth over the whole world for instant obedience, was one day informed of a ridiculous incident. A small village on a Greek island had rebelled against his authority, and had been helped by some people called Athenians, miserable worms living on the other side of the Aegean Sea. It was scarcely credible that they should so greatly dare, and the mighty Darius did not take it seriously, asking his courtiers only to remind him frequently of the name of Athens. That the presumptuous city might not go unpunished, through the King's preccupation with weightier matters.

Who were these Greeks of the islands, and who the reckless Athenians who had braved the King's wrath in a quarrel not their own?

The earliest account of the Greeks, or Hellenes, is given in two long epic poems, called *The Iliad* and *The Odyssey*, attributed to a blind poet called Homer. The Iliad tells the story of a long war fought between a confederation of Greek princes and the king of Troy, whose son had stolen the beautiful wife, Helen, of the Greek leader. Greeks and Trojans were akin in race, and coming from the Caucasus had settled on different sides of the Hellespont, Troy (or Ilium) being the older state. Troy was at last taken and destroyed, and the victorious Greeks sailed for home, to meet with many adventures and perils on the way, told in *The Odyssey*, the tale of the wanderings of Odysseus. This Odysseus had been a man of guile and cunning, who had helped much to bring victory to his friends but had earned the anger of the gods by his deceits, so he was shipwrecked and had to suffer long before he could return to his wife. Among others who befriended him was King Minos of Crete, and much is told of that centre of civilisation. Crete was called "Star of the Seas," and from it first spread a new civilisation to the West, different from that of Egypt and Asia. Cretan merchants had traded with Spain, and certain Spanish dancers still wear a costume derived from Crete in the days of Minos, before the labyrinthine palace was destroyed about 1,500 BC. Not long ago, Sir Arthur Evans dug up the wonderful Cretan palace, having shops and all within one building, really like a maze, and showing traces of having been left suddenly, when enemies destroyed the city. Cretans are said to have migrated to Tuscany, taking their arts with them, for later Tuscan fame.

Troy has also been discovered by the archaeologist Heinrich Schliemann, who first was surprised to unearth a city which did not agree with its description in *The Iliad*. No fewer than six cities were then found to be buried one under another, and one of them was just as described by Homer.

It was the descendants of these Greeks who in the fifth century BC incurred the anger of Darius, especially the men of Athens, one of the separate city states of Hellas. In due course the king despatched one of his best generals with a punitive force to subdue Athens and her friends, and bring their leaders captive to Persepolis. But the result was a still greater shock to Persian pride, for the impossible had happened—the mouse had conquered the elephant. The outraged monarch was prepared now to go in person to avenge the insult, but death stopped him from going, and his son Xerxes was a lesser man. However, to carry out his father's plan, Xerxes prepared a huge force of 200,000 men, to fight 5,000 Athenians, and sent a formidable fleet of ships, fantastic in beauty and enormous in size. He had a bridge of boats anchored across the Hellespont, that his army might cross dryshod, and had a throne prepared for him on a hillside from where he could watch the triumph of his arms.

Athens now was in great danger, and sent to other Greek states to help her, and save their common motherland and their freedom. Sparta sent 300 men to man the narrow pass of Thermopylae, and they held the Persian hosts there for three days, only one returning to Sparta. The Persians then swept on to burn Athens, but it was a barren victory, for the Athenian leaders had abandoned their city to stake all on the prowess of their ships. In the narrow Gulf of Athens the large Persian ships were at a disadvantage, and Xerxes had the mortification of seeing his magnificent fleet thoroughly beaten in the Battle of Marathon, routed and chased away in disorder.

The war between the Greeks and Persians was to last many years longer, with variable fortunes, for the Greeks could not always maintain their high heroism, or strengthen in peace the bonds of unity they had forged in the hour of danger. Nevertheless, the torch of life was now with them, and their civilisation was to grow while the Persian declined, till after two hundred years it would be the turn of the Greeks to invade and burn Persepolis. Civilisation had passed from Asia to Europe.

The Greeks had a new political idea—that of freedom. They thought it monstrous that one man should command and all have to obey. Law must be made by general agreement, and they must be respected. Every Greek was strong in his own self-respect, and when united they were invincible, whereas the Persian armies were composed of men conscripted from many subject peoples, oppressed by tyrants. Greeks too were distinguished by their intelligence, their love of literature, drama and art. They cared supremely for physical beauty and health, organising athletic contests.

17
The Hellenic Spirit: Creator of Europe

The Athenians rebuilt their city and its temples, lavishing all their wealth and artistic skill on noble architecture and civic dignity, not caring much for personal splendour. Pallas Athene, virgin goddess of wisdom and protectress of their city, was their ideal of perfection, and the sculptor Phidias was commissioned to create a statue of ivory and gold to express her perfect beauty. Phidias and Praxiteles and their pupils filled the city with marvellous statues, still taken as standards of perfection for their measurements of the human form and its proportions. The Greeks looked on physical beauty as moral, and the healthy cultivation of the human body was to them a duty owed to the gods. Athletics were organised as part of religious festivities, and laurel wreaths awarded in contests of strength and skill were as highly prized as if they had been of gold.

Athens took the lead in freedom of thought. A wise man called Socrates, leader of an intellectual circle, took to going round among the citizens asking them thought-provoking questions, as how a statue of ivory and gold could be expected to save the city from danger, and why they believed so easily the things told them by priests, instead of thinking for themselves. After some time the city council was stirred to action, and Socrates was brought to trial as a corrupter of youth. After a long trial, the votes of his enemies prevailed, and he was condemned to death by the drinking of hemlock. So many were horrified at the idea of executing so wise a man that Socrates was privately informed that he would be allowed to escape from Athens, but he refused to run away, saying that Athens had a right to demand his life, and that he would not injure her laws by evading them. So he spent his last day discussing philosophical questions with his friends, calmly drinking the poison when it was brought to him by the weeping guard, and humorously answering a query as to where he wished to be buried by saying that they would have to catch him before they could bury him, but they could do what they liked with his body.

So a critical faculty of mind was awakened, and a thirst for first-hand knowledge carried on by Plato, one of the greatest of philosophers, and by Eratosthenes, who disclosed that the world was a sphere, and Aristotle who speculated and experimented in natural science. These were great educators, whose methods we should follow today; they kindled a flame in a few that spread to the many. There was also in Athens, and in other Greek towns to a lesser extent, a birth of great literature and drama; plays of Aeschylus and Euripides were models of the Shakespearean drama, and Greek poetry and literature in general were to be copied by Latin writers, and to influence all Europe. A great inventor was Archimedes, who cogitated on the reason why he was upheld by water in swimming, and discovered the principles of weight in water, by using the eyes of imagination. He also made use of mirrors to focus the sun's rays on a hostile Roman fleet off Syracuse, so causing a fire to break out on the enemy ships. He was a great mathematician, and was studying triangles when Roman soldiers burst into his room and killed him.

The kingdom of Macedon; which was only regarded as half-Hellenic by the Greeks, rose to great power under a king called Philip, who succeeded in uniting the Greek states under his hegemony, by thrilling them with the idea of carrying out an invasion of Persia, the ancient foe. The Persian power on the Greek borders still remained a menace, chiefly because the Hellenes weakened themselves by an exhaustive war between Athens and Sparta, in which other Greek states took part as well, to the ruin of all. Macedonian encroachments had been the result, and King Philip had claimed pure Greek descent for himself, and had the wisdom to place his young son Alexander under the tutorship of the philosopher Aristotle. The Greeks now came to an agreement with Philip to fight under his leadership against Persia, on condition only that he did not rob them of their free citizenship and independence each within his own city, and to this Philip agreed.

Philip of Macedon was a great commander, having developed new arts of war, as the use of the invincible phalanx. Also he trained cavalry for us in new ways, man and horse becoming doubly strong when perfectly in union by discipline. The young prince, Alexander, when only twelve years old, was once watching these horses being trained, and burst into derisive laughter at the trainers when he saw that one ferocious horse would not suffer any rider to mount him. The trainers were offended at the child's insult, and King Philip reproved his son, saying that it took long to train a high-spirited horse; but the prince replied that he could do it at once. To cure him of boasting, the King ordered that they let him try. "Let him learn the lesson," he said, though all were alarmed. But Alexander went up to the savage horse, took his bridle and quickly jerked his head round in another direction. At once the horse became quiet and allowed the boy to mount him. Everyone thought it magical, but the boy explained that the horse had merely been frightened by its own shadow, and so had reared at the approach of a rider till his head had been turned. Alexander's mother had taught him that he was a son of Zeus or Jupiter, chief of the Greek gods, and this gave him great upliftment of soul.

Before King Philip had matured his plans for invading Persia, he was murdered at the age of forty, and Alexander inherited his throne and preparations. He was filled with a passion to conquer other countries, and to gain knowledge of the world. He took scientists and specialists of all kinds with him, engineers too for map-making, and books of poetry, drama and history for intellectual refreshment. He would discuss with his captains botany and zoology round a camp fire, and would constantly send back letters to Aristotle describing new things seen, and sending specimens. Theophrastus in Athens wrote a history of plants and animals from the material thus supplied by Alexander.

Alexander's soldiers regarded him as supernatural, and he had triumphs everywhere. After the conquest of Tyre, the Persian King tried to buy him off with the offer of half the empire, and the general Parmenius advised him to accept, but his answer was: "I would accept if I were Parmenius, but I am Alexander!" In Egypt he was welcomed as the son of Amun Ra. He entirely routed the Persian armies sent against him, burnt Persepolis, but showed courtesy to royal captives, and continued his victorious march even into India, from which he sent back to Greece descriptions of elephants and camels.

Now his soldiers were tired of travelling, and demanded to be led home; for the first time they would not be led further by him, and he raged at them, but had to give way and turn back. Still he wanted on his way home to do some more exploring—to find out whether the Persian Gulf was a lake or part of the ocean—so he sent his ships along the coast while he marched with some of his men by land. On the way he caught a fever and died, for desert travelling was very difficult, and he would not fare better than his men when they were parched with thirst.

So the empire of Alexander the Great broke up, some of his generals who had been sent to administer distant provinces soon becoming independent. Alexander had altered the face of the world, and this had been the first systematic explorative expedition in history, only to be rivalled by the second one, two hundred and fifty years later, carried out by the Roman Julius Caesar.

Romans claimed an origin akin to that of the Greeks, and it was to be their task to consolidate the world civilisation which the Greek spirit had inspired and created.

18

Man: Whither Bound

There has been revealed to us a significant unity of method in all natural building. It is clear that nature follows a plan, which is the same for atom as for planet. It was in 1924 that the embryologist Childe revealed those points of febrile activity called Physiological Gradients, not all starting together, or with the same intensity, but each to its own tempo, pursuing an independent course. To begin with, the unit cells were exactly like all the others, but through their activity they grew to differ and became specialised, for the formation of an organ, and last came the circulatory and nervous systems to link the organ with others, similarly created in independence, but to a different functional end.

These are found to be the basic principles of nature's plan:

1. The freedom and independence of organs in their several developments.
2. Development through specialisation of cells.
3. The unification of organs by the circulatory system of the flood.
4. Directive communication established by the nervous system.

Blood also consists of cells, but its substance is refuse thrown into it by the organic cells, as well as prime material taken from the outer environment. Hormones are produced by the ductless glands, and discharged into the blood-stream. They are needed to stimulate the shaping and growth of organs, which are retarded when they are insufficient. One sort of hormone is produced by the thyroid gland, and another by the liver. The blood cells called red corpuscles are just beasts of burden, to bear oxygen from the air and nourishment from food to all parts needing them. Such is the mechanism for supply of the lower physical needs; but then come into consideration the higher needs, preparing behaviour in life. In the interests of these needs, cells accomplish complete self-abnegation, transforming themselves to the nature of the function to be served. In the higher stages there is not only adaptation to work, but such a vehement force that nothing else matters; so only is specialisation achieved. Lastly, the control of the nervous system gives sensitivity and animates. Innumerable filaments from the brain link all with the psyche. An organism is no mere collection of organs. The nervous cells specialise in refinement, and one cannot conceive of one of them taking upon itself to turn starch into sugar, or fight a microbe. They imprison themselves in a closed box, the cranium, and it is not by any general election that they get their place in the governing body. The embryo can teach us the absurdity of our social mechanism, where one group claims to dominate another merely by authority, without agreement. Nature is the teacher of life—let us follow her way.

The brief review that we have taken of the history of human civilisation has been meant to show the same basic design at work, for humanity too is an organic unity that is yet being born. Like organs the different centres of civilisation have been nursed to strength in isolation, then brought into contacts by which they merged into larger organisations, or parted with what they had of value for the enrichment of despoilers before they were destroyed if they were too unadaptable to survive. Cruelties and exploitation, wars and all forms of violence have had to play their part, because men have not yet realised their common humanity and its work in fulfilment of a cosmic destiny.

World-shaking forces are now making realisation of human unity an urgent necessity. The time is past when some racial groups or nations can be civilised, leaving others servile or barbaric. Persistence in these outworn ideas can only lead to further wars and self destruction, and how can a general change of thought be effected but by the teacher; not as tyrant or missionary, but as essential leader of the rising generation? The modern teacher must be an enthusiastic student of biology, and of the psychology of the growing child, and so of the man. The "school" must mean something else than a place of instruction, where the one teaches the many, with pain on both sides—an effort carrying with it little success.

School attendance is being made everywhere compulsory—there is conscription on the educational front, a mobilisation comparable to the call made by a nation in urgent danger; but this is not a national mobilisation, but far greater, being universal, and for Life rather than Death!

Immense powers are being entrusted to teachers, who cannot evade them. As physical health should have first consideration, let us review what reforms are necessary in this respect, if teachers are to fulfil their sacred responsibility.

It is necessary in schools to record observations of every child's growth, with any aberrations from normal. Growth is not merely a harmonious increase in size, but a transformation. Man is a sculptor of himself, urged by a mysterious inner force to the attainment of an ideal determined form. Growth may be defined as a seeking after perfection, given by an impulse of life.

It is essential that civilisation should produce beautiful children. An old-fashioned dictum has been that "beauty is skin-deep", and children have been dissuaded from looking in the mirror, as smacking of sinful vanity. But we claim that schools should be institutions to help beauty, because beauty is an indication of healthy conditions of life. Good conditions induce beauty of form, and it is part of the Montessori method to achieve such harmony. We consider beauty from two points of view, the first being hereditary, and the second induced through environment.

The rate of mortality for children in their first year is enormous, quite abnormal, and due to ignorance and imperfect social conditions, not to the Will of God. The rate diminishes gradually up to the age of six, then achieving and maintaining a normal, from six to twelve years old. Those abnormal early deaths are murders, unnatural death, for which we all have to bear our share of responsibility, acknowledging ourselves criminals. After the twelfth year the rate of mortality again rises, to eighteen; it is another dangerous period, accompanying great transformation, life being only secured after eighteen.

See the victorious adult, between twenty-four and thirty-six, fitted for reproduction of life instead of for paying the toll of death. The reproductive period is actually from eighteen to forty-two, but the narrower limits for the ages of parents yield the strongest individuals who live to old age and attain fame. Children born of parents either too young or too old are often abnormal in some way, weak or wicked, other than healthy and happy children.

These statistics concern mortality, and it may be said that

the school has no concern with the dead. But every death is just a catastrophe in the midst of lesser accidents. Illness does not always bring death at once, and the high mortality among children under six is an indication of a very great number of ill children. For every dead child there must be at least a hundred sick children, partially overcome by illness. It is when the resistance of the organs is overcome that we fall ill, and for one overcome, many are on the verge of so being. Thus large numbers of children in our schools, below six and again especially from twelve to eighteen, are weak and predisposed to illness, a fact which should be appreciated by educators.

It is an error to expect hard work, diligence and unimpeachable progress during the age of puberty. Indulgence should be shown to those who lag at this time. The life of man is whole in its length, like a cord. Touched in one part, the whole length vibrates, so there may be far-reaching consequences in adult life to some occurrence that seemed trivial in childhood, and as unfavourable happenings are likely during these weakened stages, the teacher's responsibility is great towards humanity.

Pedagogical anthropology has made great strides in Europe and America recently. In Italy prisoners have been studied, and found usually to have malformations of the physical form. Is the ugly man a criminal? A murderer or thief is seldom different from other children at birth, but conditions are such that they cannot adapt themselves to the laws of their country. Social conditions act on body and mind, and the individual becomes abnormal; the criminal usually reflects the errors of society. Very rarely are criminals born, so it is easy to erase criminality from the world, if only we understand and make the effort. The physical form is the exponent of the whole circumstance which produces the criminal.

It is also found that the greatest number of malformations is among the insane, who seldom inherit insanity. There are millions of insane today, and the numbers are increasing, but it has been proved not to be hereditary, so it will diminish if the child is scientifically studied and given proper care.

Tuberculosis is a terrible scourge, as also rickets, heart disease and many other bodily deformities, once thought wrongly to be hereditary. The chest of the tubercular patient is abnormally narrow, and the defect could have been remedied by right exercise in childhood. The study of Bacteriology has diminished infectious diseases, and the time has come when scientific care of children should be regarded as a social prophylaxis without which it is vain to judge things from a moral standpoint. Certain physical deformities have proved to be common in every class of life, rich and poor alike, and amusingly enough the schools themselves have been indicted as responsible for some of them. But cures adopted were sometimes worse than the disease; it was as if they would start to straighten children's backs by hanging them with weights on their legs in resting periods, while making them sit most of their time with backs bent over a desk. Similarly at the end of the last century it was discovered that it was bad for children to sit in closed rooms with poor lighting that produced myopia, and the remedy was to give spectacles to children of eight.

The child's history has been terrible. We can laugh at these remedies today, but at least they began to open windows and let in more air, and since the panacea for curvature of the spine was thought to be intervals for straightening the spine after an hour's rest, the principle of frequent rest from work was established. No such possibility was yet conceived as a happy education of children, so still many had to be sacrificed to civilisation, and the best they could do was to compromise, reducing hours in instruction to the minimum, cutting out from the curriculum grammar, geometry and algebra, making outside play obligatory and postponing the age for entry into school. But however much free periods have been increased and children urged to play rather than study, strangely the children have remained mentally fatigued notwithstanding all these reforms. Montessori schools have proved that the child needs a cycle of work for which he has been mentally prepared; such intelligent work with interest is not fatiguing, and he should not be arbitrarily cut off from it by a call to play. Interest is not immediately born, and if when it has been created the work is withdrawn, it is like depriving a whetted appetite of the food that will satisfy it.

Through long experimentation we have now arrived at much elimination of error, and the possession of a key which can unlock for children the gates of a healthy and happy education. On our courage and perseverance in its use depends the future of humanity.

19

Conclusion

The individual treads the path of life, beset with dangers on all sides. Life is a veritable battle-front; one may come through, but be crippled or scarred with suffering by the time he enters the peaceful phase of life, and should be the triumphant adult. Then he comes under the protection of society, which takes the place of his former guardians, and provides him with the means of living and with a mate. Together now they tread the way of life, climbing to their unknown destiny, and before they descend they will leave behind them the fruits of their love. In their decline they separate; the downward march is solitary, and they pass into oblivion.

Society considers important the period of ascents, when they are building monuments of their actions, and all rewards go to the triumphant and successful. The privileged classes are the care and concern of society, despite the French Revolution and others. The poor have not yet had proper consideration, and there always remains one class that is yet more completely ignored, even among the rich. Such is childhood! All social problems are considered from the point of view of the adult and his needs—housing, unemployment, wages, suffrage, etc. Far more important are the needs of the child, in whom there exist forces that may remain curbed or may now be developed as has not before been widely possible. It is not enough to ensure for the child food, clothing and shelter; on the satisfaction of his more spiritual needs the progress of humanity depends—the creation indeed of a stronger and better humanity.

The social problems of the child and the adult are therefore integrated, but can also be separately considered, and the school bears special responsibility for the child. Youth is universally recruited in the school for the great army of life. The potentialities of a cultivated humanity should be the root of every social question, but the adult is beyond reform, and experiments with him repeatedly fail. He is a tough subject, to set in his mould for the revelation of new human possibilities. We delude ourselves on having reached great heights of philanthropy with our miserable crumbs of social charity, but even such are doled out to adults only. To some food, to some an unemployment dole, to others the privilege of free speech; none of these panacea do much to better or improve social ills.

Suppose we set up in schools the same social improvements that we are so proud of achieving. Let us feed the children, give them playgrounds, clothing, freedom of speech (the right to freely ask questions of the teacher). These small things will be a beginning, but will not suffice, and to learn what greater remedies are needed, we must study the nature of humanity, as revealed in the first years of life. Then we will know with certainty what is needed, and we will also know that the remedies can be far more effectively applied to the child than to the adult.

There is certainly a difference between those who are starved, naked and silenced, and those who are thriving, glad and outspoken, but this difference is not enough. It is only through science and through the illuminated personality that the world remedy will come—not by giving a morsel of food or a rag of clothing, nor even by gift of a franchise.

There is something which humanity lacks fundamentally, and it is to be sought in the very origin of life. There alone can be found the key.

It has been assumed throughout this book, that teachers taking Montessori classes of the advanced type will previously have been familiar with the primary course, in which psychology plays necessarily a bigger part in preparation for the whole method. So there has been less emphasis here on the attitude expected of the teacher towards the children in his or her care, and some concluding reminders may not be out of order.

In the advanced as in the primary stage, the first step to take in order to become a Montessori teacher is to shed omnipotence and to become a joyous observer. If the teacher can really enter into the joy of seeing things being born and growing under his own eyes, and can clothe himself in the garment of humility, many delights are reserved for him that are denied to those who assume infallibility and authority in front of a class. Such teachers suffer from illusions, being far from the truth. They agree that it is necessary to cultivate the will in children, for spontaneous interest, but contend that it must be strictly controlled and restrained. That is a contradiction in terms; you cannot develop by repression. Unfortunately logic does not function in people who suffer from illusions, so these teachers enter the school and begin to carry out their contradictions. They do the easiest thing—repress, command, destroy. Destruction is easily and quickly done, whether the structure is simple or complex; anyone can do it. But how difficult it is to construct.

The old-fashioned teacher subconsciously made an

exaltation of his own virtues. He was perfect, in the sense of knowing what should be done and what left undone. He had empty beings in front of him to be filled with facts, and created morally in his own likeness—God help them! Those beings who still had in their souls another far greater creator were forced to resemble the teacher, who was resolved to mould them to his model of "goodness" or punish them for disobedience. Such a teacher is not even a tyrant, for it takes intelligence to become a tyrant, after the historical precedent.

Obedience is no mechanical thing, but a natural force of social cohesion, intimately related to the will, even its sublimation. At first sight this statement may astonish, but it is true. Obedience of the right kind is a sublimation of the individual's will, a quality in the human soul without which society could not exist. But an obedience without true self-control, an obedience which is not the consequence of an awakened and exercised will, brings whole nations to disaster.

The teacher then makes his great renunciation of power and authority, to find himself immensely the gainer by their loss. He achieves the patience of the scientist, a patience which is rather intense interest in watching. Scientists too renounce things which human beings usually find attractive, but they waste few regrets on them. We remember Madame Curie, who felt only annoyance when some university wanted to interrupt her work on radium to confer on her an honorary degree. Edison too, one of the first friends of the Montessori Method, was soon weary of being dragged by a fashionable wife to social functions, when his heart was in his laboratory. One day on return he tore off his tie and dress-suit, tied them in a bundle and threw them out of the window, exclaiming "There goes your social husband!"—

to resume an old dressing-gown and slippers for work. People like these counted it no sacrifice to renounce lesser for greater joys. They did what they liked best to do, having acquired an intense interest which transformed and ennobled them, and the teacher who reaches this stage of interest is similarly transformed. He or she joins the happy group of men who have taken the road of life. As surely as the scientists they penetrate life's secrets, and win its rewards, not only for themselves but for all.